HANCOCK'S
HALF HOUR

First published in Great Britain in 1974 by
THE WOBURN PRESS
67 Great Russell Street
London WC1B 3BT

ISBN 0 7130 0087 2

The publishers acknowledge with thanks the
co-operation of the BBC.

Co-ordinating editors: Colin Webb and
Kate Dunning
Art editing and design by Lawrence Edwards

Printed and Bound in Great Britain by
Butler & Tanner Ltd.

HANCOCK'S HALF HOUR

Written by
Ray Galton
and
Alan Simpson

*with an Introduction
by Peter Black*

THE WOBURN PRESS

CONTENTS

Introduction   page 7
by Peter Black

The Missing Page   page 11
first broadcast
Friday 26th February 1960

The Reunion Party   page 33
first broadcast
Friday 4th March 1960

I think the world
is both funny and sad,
which seem to me
to be the two
basic ingredients of
good comedy.
The character I play
isn't a character
I put on and off
like a coat.
It is a part of me
and a part of
everybody else I see.
The secret of
my work is a knowledge
of what constitutes
living in general,
I think. You take
the weaknesses of your
own character and of
other people's characters
and you exploit them.
You show yourself up,
and you show them up.

Tony Hancock
speaking to John Freeman
on *Face to Face*

Hancock Alone   page 57
first broadcast
Friday 26th May 1961

The Blood Donor   page 99
first broadcast
Friday 23rd June 1961

The Bowmans   page 77
first broadcast
Friday 2nd June 1961

Ray Galton and Alan Simpson   page 125
in conversation with Colin Webb

PUBLISHER'S NOTE

In order to re-create in book form what was the 'essential Hancock', we have avoided using production stills and instead have prepared over two hundred frame blow-ups from the original films. Due to the line formulation of television pictures there has been, inevitably, a reduction of quality in photographic reproduction. However, the result clearly records the genius of Tony Hancock, which here combines with the words of Galton and Simpson to produce a permanent record of perhaps the most successful and memorable television comedy series.

The interaction of pictures and text has been achieved by the careful art editing of the designer, Lawrence Edwards. We are grateful for the assistance and co-operation given to Mr Edwards by the staff of the BBC Film Library, where the frames were selected. Acknowledgement is due to the following for their permission to reproduce copyright material: BBC Enterprises for all the photographs which accompany the scripts; the BBC for the photograph on page 128 and those on the back cover; Michael Busselle for his photographs of Galton and Simpson; Jonathan Cape Ltd. for the extracts from *Face to Face;* the *Radio Times* for three of the photographs on the back cover; Rex Features Ltd. for the photograph on page 133.

INTRODUCTION

by Peter Black

During the seven years 1954 — 1961 the character created by Tony Hancock and the writers Ray Galton and Alan Simpson became the most popular and admired comedian in the land. At his peak, in his 1961 television series, he was reaching a third of the population — a huge figure when we remember that the BBC was still fighting to win back some of the numbers it had lost to the ITV network. Better than Hancock's ratings was the quality of his success. Like all the great comedians he appealed to all levels. The depth and truth in his comedy went far below the surface joke of the funny man in baggy suits and astrakhan collar. The BBC recognised this by inviting Hancock to play the classic part of Gogol's Government Inspector. John Freeman, at the time a celebrated television interviewer of those who were eminent and interesting, invited Hancock to be opened up in his penetrating series, 'Face to Face'. The recognition that Hancock was something exceptional lasted to the end of his life, and explained why when things began to go wrong for him and he was placing himself beyond the reach of rescue, he never lost the affectionate concern he had earned. The public saw in his decline — by a fateful symmetry it lasted another seven years — the presence of authentic tragedy. When he died in 1968 the Hancock of the great achievement had already died. Let me recall how great it was.

He was born in Birmingham in 1924. When he was three the family moved to Bournemouth, where his father was successful enough as publican and part-time entertainer to send him to boarding and then public school. When he was 15, the war broke out. He decided he had had enough of school, a decision which may have been right for the stagestruck boy he was but which, typically, the man he became regretted, feeling that his education had been incomplete.

The comic Hancock creation spent the war parachuting behind the German lines, driving his tank single-handed for Berlin, leading daring submarine raids on Nazi battleship bases. The real Hancock joined the R.A.F., shifted to entertainment, and toured the fronts for three years with Ralph Reader's Number Nine Gang Show. When peace came he had his share of the touring comedian's world of tatty digs, sharp-tongued landladies and vile food, eventually taking his turn as resident comic at the Windmill. He got into radio, in the early Fifties still the country's biggest and most popular source of entertainment, by way of 'Workers' Playtime', a modest lunch-time variety session aimed at factory canteen lunch-breaks, and 'Happy Go Lucky', a series with the comedian Derek Roy. This was important for him because he met Roy's writers, the two very young newcomers Galton and Simpson, both aged twenty.

In 1950 Hancock shot to the top in 'Educating Archie', a comedy series built round the dummy created by the ventriloquist Peter Brough. Roy Speer, its producer, had spotted a quality in Hancock that marked him from others; he was more of a comic actor than a straight comedian. Speer brought him in as tutor to Archie, the supposed schoolboy. In this part Hancock was not the first, but he was the best, responding to scripts (by Eric Sykes) in which he was a teacher who felt that the job of instructing a wooden dummy was beneath him. The beginnings of the Hancock creation, with its seedy grandiloquence and boastful, dashed pretensions, appeared here. Hancock had arrived. And as so often happens to entertainers (actors are luckier because the public does not expect to see them in more than one play at a time) he was promptly and recklessly overworked.

Jack Hylton signed him up for a twice-nightly revue in London and Blackpool, and though Hancock came to dread the repetition, and hoisted distress signals by drinking noticeably too much, they seem to have gone unnoticed. His managers let him carry on with twice-nightly revue until 1956. Thereafter he was able to concentrate on 'Hancock's Half Hour', which had established a huge success on radio and was about to take him to a success on TV beyond anything he or his writers could have dreamed of.

Galton and Simpson had begun to write for him in 'Calling All Forces'. In 1954 the three of them were ready for the so far unattempted adventure of trying comedy about people, with a story that would run half an hour without musical interludes, guest stars, gags, funny voices and catchphrases. In the beginning it could not altogether give up the last two, simply because the certain laugh they got couldn't be thrown away overnight. But the qualities that would make the series grow were there from the start, though they had to wait for television, slower and closer to the pace of real life, before they blossomed into the richly natural comedy everyone remembers.

The essential quality of Hancock, Galton and Simpson was that they held a consistent point of view about the world and wanted their work to express it. It was never enough just to get a laugh. They shared a view of comedy as rooted in an honest, rueful, sympathetic stare at reality, which Hancock's whole career was a steady process of examining and refining. He and they saw the funny side of yearning and failure. From his beginning to his end he retained in his theatre act the bad impersonations of film stars as done by a ham who didn't know they were bad. He loved old actor jokes, stories of disasters brazened out, of indignities heaped on the dignified, of the blustering self-confidence

that was leaking away inside. None of us has ever bought a car, planned a holiday, got married, ordered a meal, played a sport, and so on without end, without doing at least some of them in the Hancock style of putting a brave face on a hopeless situation while keeping absolutely unshaken the conviction that it's all a ridiculous mistake, we aren't that kind of person at all. It is the comic fantasy at the heart of golf, a game kept going by every bad player's belief that he's a good one who, for some reason he can't explain, is off his game that day, though he'll be on it tomorrow. And this self-deception is the basis of the oldest and funniest of man's consoling jokes. Hancock brought to it the sharpness that kept pathos at bay. There was never a touch of pathos about Hancock's performance. He was an aggressive, vainglorious mug, redeemed by a defiant stoicism.

How much of the character was in the man? He was in the three of them. Galton and Simpson shared his vision of the comic, revered writers and comedians who enlarged it — Sid Field, W. C. Fields, Will Hay, James Thurber, Stephen Leacock (a fertiliser of every one of the better writing talents in broadcasting comedy) and, at first without knowing it, Dickens, from whom they borrowed the use of fantastic, unexpected, precise imagery. 'Models, all bones and salt cellars.' 'I've got toes like globe artichokes.'

Hancock the character's cultural allusions came from Galton and Simpson's own frenzied catching up on their reading in the sanatorium where they had met as TB patients. Hancock the person used to shut himself in his room struggling to take in Kant. They were all eternally amused by the same joke, the collapse of the grand into the ungrammatical and baffled. As the following scripts so abundantly illustrate, they built a whole person, inflated and coloured by a funny, melancholy, outrageous clown who served and was nourished by two exceptionally gifted young writers.

The TV scripts retained at first the radio characters created by Hancock and Sid James. It was never quite clear what Hancock was supposed to be. His life support system — sometimes he was a ham actor, sometimes a would-be councillor, sometimes an old Desert

Rat — was left as vague as Mr Pickwick's. Sid James, a South African actor with a seamed and craggy face that everyone liked, was the earthy realist, short of any kind of culture, a crudely materialistic deflator of Hancock's aspirations for a more noble life. Here they are in 'The Reunion Party'. Hancock is awaiting three old comrades from the War. Sid deplores this morbid clinging to the past:

Tony It's not a question of clinging to the past. It was the wonderful feeling we had in those days. A bunch of young chaps, thrown together from all walks of life, were joined together with a sense of purpose, mutual respect . . .

Sid Well I don't know what sort of regiment you were in mate, but it wasn't like that in mine. As soon as the shells started coming over we disintegrated. First bloke on the motor bike was off, never mind about the others.

Tony Well it wasn't like that with us. It was one for all and all for one . . . Beautiful friendships were formed in those days, born in the heat of battle, and forged in the plonk bars of Cairo. The four of us, like quads we were . . . Smudger Smith, Ginger Johnson, Chalky White and me.

Sid Kippers Hancock.

Tony How did you know they called me Kippers?

Sid With your feet what else could they call you?

Tony The condition of my feet in those days was quite different to what they are today. Chasing the Hun across Europe, that was what flattened these, mate . . . as far as I'm concerned, my feet represent a war wound.

And on it goes, laconic, quiet lines without a gag in them, two men talking in the living room, the laughter welling unforced out of character reacting to situation. The series

ran until 1961. Then Hancock decided it was time to move on from Railway Cuttings, East Cheam, and the James—Hancock characters. Some show business writers simplified his motives into one of the Hollywood backstage musical plots — boy meets boy, they make good, one becomes a star and ditches the other. The only resemblance between the myth and the facts was in the star's growing reliance on drink as comforter and unwinder. He insisted there was nothing left to say about East Cheam. He did not want to stay fixed as half a double act — not because he was vain, as the myth implied, but because he was a creative artist driven by the itch to stretch his talent. He went on to prove that his judgment was quite right. The series he made on his own, the last that Galton and Simpson wrote for him, contained the best comedy he ever did.

I suppose most of us would pick 'The Blood Donor' as the best of the best. It had a very neat, circular plot. (As with all their most successful scripts the writers had thought of the ending first.) Hancock volunteered to give some blood, complacently learned that his was from a very rare group, fainted as the needle went in, revived to have a fatuously learned conversation with Hugh Lloyd as another donor, drove the doctor crazy by telephoning to ask who'd been given his blood, finally had it put back in himself after gashing his hand on a bread knife. The complete Hancock—Galton—Simpson creation was in it. And if I had to choose a passage that illustrated the hopeful, truculent, blusterer and the writers' gift for finding the sudden, vivid, unexpected, ludicrous mental image, I could pick no better than the following:

Doctor I've just taken a small sample to test.

Tony A sample? How much do you want then?

Doctor A pint, of course.

Tony A pint? Have you gone raving mad? Oh, well, of course . . . I mean, you must be joking.

Doctor A pint is a perfectly normal quantity to take.

Tony You don't seriously expect me to believe that. I mean, I came in here in all good faith to help my country. I don't mind giving a reasonable amount, but a pint . . . why that's very nearly an armful. I'm sorry. I'm not walking around with an empty arm for anybody . . . No, I'm sorry, I've been misinformed, I've made a mistake . . . I'll do something else, I'll be a traffic warden.

Those who saw it will not read these lines without hearing the voice and seeing his face. His physical presence was so right for the words that it is impossible to imagine the scripts ever being revived with some sub-Hancockian comedian playing his part. Indeed, when we come to consider the ending to it all, it is impossible not to wonder if the long and close involvement of the man with the character was a major cause of it.

In real life Hancock was a serious, untidy, introspective person, sometimes marvellous fun to be with but too much of a worrier, a sensitive perfectionist, to enjoy his success. He never thought of himself as successful. He didn't like himself very much. He believed he was unattractive and awkward. He identified with the quarry, never with the hunters. His huge earnings worried his sense of social justice. Too often his escape from anxieties and tensions was by way of the bottom of an upturned glass; the strings of girls, fast cars, yachts and racehorses were never for him, except as part of the comic world he and his writers had built. He had an unshakable sense of general doom.

Accepting what everyone concerned with his career agreed, that the scripts were to a very large extent *about* Hancock, one can imagine the effect on a man of his temperament of this prolonged and searching examination. It is not surprising that in addition to the normally mixed feelings of the actor about writers (part gratitude for the words, part resentment against seeming to be their creature) he should have felt that they were moving in and taking possession. Seven years! Given the concentrated stare of a half-hour

script they amount to another lifetime. This is why I could never see in his break with Galton and Simpson the vanity suggested by the myth. It could have been a desperate wrench to recover himself.

The fact is he paid a price for doing the Hancock we remember. He had his share of bad luck. He was unlucky to have got himself trapped in the destructive theatre revues. His marriage was unlucky, for his wife (who was unluckier still) soon gave up hope of controlling his drinking and joined him at it, according to his biographers* in the only book about him that we have.

We might add that he was unlucky to be one of the handful that cannot use drink sensibly. He was unlucky to have succeeded so hugely in television, a medium that depends on repetition to entertain an audience that always prefers what it had last time. I know no writer and performer who has not been urged to repeat a success and discouraged from trying anything new — including Galton and Simpson, whose 'Steptoe and Son' about a pair of junk men was really a reworking of the James—Hancock situation, deeper and more realistic because it was written for actors.

Finally, he was unlucky that when he tried to move on he wasn't successful, partly because he never found writers who could light him up as splendidly as Galton and Simpson, partly because the drinking had begun to eat away at his performance. When I last saw him, in a one-man show from the Festival Hall, London, he seemed badgered, frustrated, as though his mind would no longer obey his will. He seemed to know that the drive to perfect his talent had gone too far wrong for him to be able to get it back. When he killed himself in Australia in 1968, he was only 44 but the news evoked more pity than shock.

His memorial is in this selection of scripts, from a total of 101 for radio and 59 for TV. To read them more than ten years after their first performances is to rediscover with joy that Galton and Simpson when still in their early twenties were writing some of the most gloriously funny low comedy in the language. It is not given to television to create immortals; but here in these pages a fine comedian, one of our finest, still lives.

* Freddie Hancock and David Nathan, *Hancock*, London 1969

THE MISSING PAGE

Fade up the inside of a public library. We see from the sign on the outside of the glass door at the entrance that it is the East Cheam Public Library. Tony enters, carrying a pile of books. He goes up to the Librarian's desk and puts them down.

Tony Good morrow, good curator.

Librarian Oh it's you. Overdue again. Seven reminders I've sent out to you.

Tony My dear good fellow one cannot rush one's savouring of the classics of world literature. Rome wasn't built in a day, and it's decline and fall can't be read in one.

Librarian You haven't got Gibbon's *Decline and Fall* there.

Tony That's got nothing to do with it. I've got the love lives of the Caesars here, that tells me everything . . . and between you and me, I'm not surprised it declined and fell after that lot. Kindly shove the cards back in the sockets and give me the tickets.

The Librarian goes through the books and looks inside the covers.

Librarian How have you got all these books? How many tickets have you got?

Tony Two fiction and two non-fiction.

Librarian That's four tickets. There's ten books here.

Tony Yes well, Dolly was on last time.

Librarian Do you mean Miss Hargreaves?

Tony She may be Miss Hargreaves to you, but to people who she reckons she is Dolly. And to me she is Dolly. And she always lets me have a few over the odds.

Librarian That's three and eight to pay on this lot.

'Good morrow, good curator'

Tony Three and eight? I don't want to buy 'em.

Librarian Well don't take so many out if you can't read them all in time. There are other people who want to borrow these books you know.

Tony I can't think why. A bigger load of old rubbish I haven't clapped my reading glasses on in years.

Librarian Then why did you take them out?

Tony Well there's not much choice in here, is there? I suppose *Lolita's* still out.

Librarian Yes.

Tony I thought so.

Librarian There's twenty-five thousand other books to choose from.

Tony I've read them all. I've been coming in here since I was six years old and I've read *Biggles Flies East* twenty-seven times . . . I'm not wading through that again.

Librarian *(handing him a leaflet)* There's a list of our latest additions. And one book one ticket. I'm not Dolly.

Tony All right then. Come on, give me my tickets.

Librarian Not till you've paid your fine. Three and eight.

Tony Disgusting . . . they're even taxing learning these days.

He gets the money out. The Librarian is examining a book, and points to a page in it.

Librarian Did you do this?

Tony No I didn't. I don't like eggs. And you needn't examine the corners of the pages, I don't bend them over. I use bookmarks. I use a piece of ribbon off my chocolate box.

Librarian Yes, well take it out.

He hands him a book with a piece of ribbon sticking out. Tony takes the book, opens it, and all the pages fall out all over the floor. The Librarian watches all this in silence.

Tony It's nothing to do with me.

Librarian You've been bending the books round backwards, haven't you? That's going to cost you another seven and six.

Tony I'm not paying for bad workmanship.

Librarian Do you know how to read a book?

Tony Yes of course I do.

Librarian You hold it like this.

He opens a book and holds it in a reading position.

Librarian You rest it in your hand like that. You don't bend it back like this . . .

He bends it back and all the pages fall out.

Tony Touché. Stand by with your date stamping machine. I shall return.

He goes over to the book shelves. There are some people looking for books, others sitting down at the reference table. All is quiet. Big notices reading 'SILENCE' are hanging up. As he passes the reference table . . .

Tony   Morning.

The readers look up and angrily shush him.

Tony   Charming. I was only passing the . . .

They shush him again.

Tony   Oh come now, after all . . .

Renewed 'sshhhs' from the readers.

Tony   Yes but . . .

They all shush him. A little man who hasn't been joining in now looks up from his book and shushes all the people who have been shushing Tony.

Tony   Quite right too. If you must sshhh don't sshhh so loud.

Little Man   *(to Tony)* Ssshhh!

Tony   Oh shut up.

A man standing by the book shelves turns round.

Man *(very loudly)* Quiet please.

Everybody turns and shushes him. Tony goes over to the shelves. A woman is choosing a book from the Crime section. Tony stops and looks at the title. He shakes his head, pulls out another book, and hands it to her. Gives her the thumbs up and carries on. He stops a little further on and starts examining the titles on the Crime shelves. He apparently can't find what he's looking for so he moves on to the next section which is marked 'Greek Philosophy'. He starts searching for some books, then snaps his fingers and beckons. The Librarian comes up.

Librarian Can I help you?

Tony Yes, I'm looking for Sir Charles Bestead's complete history of the Holy Byzantine Empire.

Librarian *(impressed)* Oh, you want to borrow it?

Tony Yes please.

Librarian I'm so pleased. We don't get much call for it. I'm so pleased there are still men of culture left. It's a magnificent edition.

Tony Oh yes, yes, most useful.

Librarian I do hate to see it neglected.

Tony Oh I often borrow it, I find it most helpful.

Librarian I think I've misjudged you, haven't I? Is there anything else I can get for you?

Tony Yes er . . . Plato's *Republic,* the complete translation of Homer's *Iliad,* and Ulbricht's *Roman Law* . . . The Wilkinson edition of course.

Librarian Of course. A very wise choice. You've chosen probably the four best books in the library.

Tony I agree . . . have you got them?

Librarian Of course, I'll get them.

Librarian *(going off)* The first time in four years there's been any call for these.

He finds the four volumes, all great big books about six inches thick. He goes back to Tony.

Librarian There we are. It's times like this that make my job worth while.

Tony Thank you very much, they're the ones.

Librarian You can have all these on one ticket.

Tony Oh, that's most kind of you.

He puts them on the floor at the Crime section, then stands on them, stretches up, and takes down a book from a higher shelf.

Tony Ah, that's the little beauty I'm after. *Lady Don't fall Backwards. (He steps off the books)* Thank you very much. I won't need those any more for now. Keep them handy though, they're just the right height.

The Librarian picks up the books lovingly.

'Bertrand Russell,
didn't he write Kiss the
Blood off my Hands?'

'Of course he didn't
. . . you're thinking of
Aldous Huxley'

Librarian *(with passion)* You barbarian!
You're illiterate you are, ignorant and
illiterate.

*The readers turn on them and shush them
loudly.*

Tony You see what you've done now, you've
set them off again. Go on — be about your
business, you highly-strung fool.

The Librarian goes off in a huff.

Tony Really, these beatniks are becoming
impossible.

*He turns back to the book shelves and studies
the titles, then takes another couple of books.
He moves a pile along and we see Sid's face*

looking through from the other side.

Sid Hallo.

Tony Oh cor . . . *(Has a turn)* What are you
doing here? Oh dear, you frightened the life
out of me.

Sid I thought I'd come and see what it was
all about. All this book business. So I've come
to get some books out.

Tony You've never read a book in your life.
Don't give me that. You've run one yes, but
you've never read one.

Sid No straight up. I joined today. I thought
I'd see what it's all about, so I've come round
here.

'Shhh-h'

**'Sid please, not in here . . .
no punch ups
on municipal property'**

Tony And straight to the Crime section. I expect you're looking for some new ideas aren't you.

Sid Well you're looking at the Crime section as well.

Tony That is neither here or there. I read thrillers purely as relaxation between the heavy stuff. I find fifty pages of *Dead Dames Don't Talk* the perfect hors-d'oeuvre to an all night bash at Bertrand Russell.

Sid Bertrand Russell, didn't he write *Kiss the Blood off my Hands?*

Tony *Kiss the Blood off my Hands.* Bertie of all people. Of course he didn't. That's not his style at all. You're thinking of Aldous Huxley.

Sid Well there's nothing round here. Anything round your side?

Tony There's one or two things that might appeal to you.

Sid Hang on.

Sid disappears and then comes round the end of the bookshelf and joins Tony.

Sid Let's have a look then. *(He selects a book)* What about this one? Smashing cover.

He laughs raucously and a reader turns and shushes them.

Sid *(to the reader)* Who are you shushing? Are you looking for a mouthful of signet rings?

17

Tony Sid please, not in here . . . no punch ups on municipal property.

Sid Well, I'm not taking that . . . you heard him shushing me, I wasn't doing anything.

Tony *(whispers)* He's entitled to, you're not supposed to make a noise in a public library.

Sid Oh all right·then, but he'd better watch it.

Tony Yes all right. Give us your book.

He looks at it. The following dialogue is in loud whispers.

Tony I've read it.

Sid What's it like?

Tony Not very good. I wouldn't bother.

Sid Yeah, but what's it about? What happens?

Tony Well you see, this bird is in the room with this bloke and suddenly the door's flung open and her husband walks in and . . .

The readers turn round and shush them. Tony now mimes the action of the book to Sid, with Sid reacting appropriately. Tony describes the girl's shape, then a man with big shoulders, does the lover kissing her passionately. Jumps back, opens a door and does melodramatic step into the room as the husband with the melodramatic 'Ah ha'. The husband and the lover have a terrific fight, strangling each other, etc. Finally the husband draws a gun

and shoots the lover several times. Does the lover doing the death scene, then, as husband, kicks the body and jumps on it. Then does the girl pleading on her knees. The husband throws her on one side. Has a struggle with the gun and the gun gets forced against her and it goes off. Another big death scene from the girl. She dies. The husband is remorseful. He tries to revive her. He jumps up and puts hand to ear. He turns round and puts hands up as the police come in the door. Holds out his hands for handcuffs. Next Tony imitates the judge sitting at the bench. Describes the wig with his hands, bows to three sides of the court, raps gavel three times, then does advocate pleading the case. Puts black cap on and grabs back of collar to indicate being strung up. By now the Librarian has come onto the scene and has watched the last half of this pantomime. Tony suddenly realises he is there and, with great embarrassment, busies himself selecting some book.

Librarian   What do you think you're doing?

Tony   And just what do you mean by that?

Librarian   This is a library, not the Royal Academy of Dramatic Art. I've been watching you. You've been creating a disturbance ever since you came in here.

Tony   I was merely trying to describe to my friend what his book is about.

Librarian   We get a thousand people a day in here, supposing they all did it? A thousand people, all gesticulating. We can't have that in a public library.

Tony   I was not gesticulating.

Librarian   You were gesticulating . . . And there have been complaints. It's most distracting. You'd better get your books stamped up and leave.

Sid   Just a minute mate, don't you tell me what to do, mate. You're trying it on with the wrong kiddy . . . just don't tell me what to do. I'm not the type.

One of the readers shushes loudly. Sid stalks over to the reading table.

Sid   Who did that? Come on, who shushed? Who was it?

Tony   *(restraining him)* Sid, come away. Don't start anything. You're always showing me up. *(To the readers)* I do apologize, it's not his fault, he can't stand rules and regulations. It's the gipsy in him. Come on, back to your caravan, I'll buy you a new pair of earrings.

He escorts Sid reluctantly over to the counter, where the Librarian stamps the books and hands them to him.

Librarian   There's your books. Back in fourteen days, or I shall ask you to turn in your tickets.

Tony   *(pointed)* Very well, but I might warn you, the Chairman of the Library Committee

is a member of the same lodge as me, if you get what I mean. *(Makes a Mason's sign)* Once a moose always a moose. Just watch it, eh?

Sid and Tony leave the counter.

Tony   That's frightened the daylights out of him.

As they go out of the door a woman comes in carrying a book. Tony has a quick look at the title, then yells into the library.

Tony   *Lolita's* back!

All the people round the reading table jump up and make a dignified rush to the counter for the book.

Man   I believe you'll find I'm top of the list . . .

Woman   No, no I had my name down before it was published.

Fade on a heated argument between the readers and the Librarian.
Fade up Tony's flat. He is sitting at a table reading Lady Don't Fall Backwards, *fully engrossed in the book. He reacts to what he is reading — it is obviously something rather horrific and very tense. He stops and has a drink of water, and carries on reading. Meanwhile, Sid finishes his book and closes it.*

Sid   Well . . . if that's reading books, I'm going back to the telly. What a load of codswallop. *The Stranglers of Bolton.* They should have strangled the bloke who wrote it. *(Looks at the cover)* Grant Peabody. How can you write books with a name like that?

Tony   Do you mind? I'm trying to read. Don't interrupt. I'm on the edge of my seat here.

Sid   Good is it?

Tony   Good? It's red hot, mate. I hate to think of this sort of book getting in the wrong

hands. As soon as I've finished this, I shall recommend they ban it.

Sid   As good as that is it? What's it about then?

Tony   It's a murder mystery. With loads of girls in it, and they've all fallen for the private eye, you see, and they're all rich and they're all beautiful and he's got a big white American car. Oh dear, it's the sort of life you dream about. He's good looking, quick repartee, judo, marvellous apartment, all the birds. Well

I'm finished with The Saint after this. I'm a Johnny Oxford man from now on. This is marvellous, twenty-five murders so far, the New York Police don't know what's going on at all, the D.A.'s been in to see the Governor, cause it's political as well, you see, anyway this Jocelyn Knockersbury, a typist at UNO, has been done in and the plans stolen, along with the seating arrangement at the peace conference. Since which time another twenty-four have been done in . . .

Sid   What, all UNO typists?

Tony   Yes, twenty-five of them . . . *(Reads a bit more)* Hallo . . . another one's gone. Ooh what a nasty way to go. Someone poured water over her electric typewriter. Well this is a mystery. Who's behind it all? Who's the murderer? Now the bloke I suspected is in Salt Lake City, it can't be him. Do you know, I've been wrong on every page so far. Every time I suspect someone, they get killed. I can't wait to get to the end of this . . . it's going to be a complicated ending, this one.

Sid Yeah, well hurry up and finish it, it's getting late. Have a look at the last page.

Tony You can't do that. It makes the whole thing pointless, you might as well not read it. It's like looking at the next card when you're playing snap. Please do be quiet, I've read the same sentence three times. Hallo, he's found something. It's all right, Johnny knows who did it. He's found a ginger hair on her skirt. He's solved it! He's narrowed his eyes and a little smile has flickered across his face. He always does that when he knows something.

Sid Well come on then, who done it?

Tony It'll be on the last page. He always keeps you in suspense till the last page this bloke. *(Reads on, getting more excited)* Yes I thought so, he's invited everybody into his

flat. He always does that. He lashes them up with drinks, lights a cigarette and explains who did it. Then the murderer rushes to the window, slips and falls, hits the pavement, and Johnny Oxford turns round to the guests, finishes his Manhattan and says, 'New York is now a cleaner place to live in'. The End. Turn over, a list of new books and an advert for skinny blokes.

Sid If you always know what's going to happen, why bother to read it?

Tony Because I don't know who it is who's going to hit the pavement. Now please keep quiet, Johnny's just started his summing up, prior to unmasking the murderer. *(He concentrates on the book, making odd noises as he notes the points being made)* Oh so she was in on it, the one I told you about. She said she'd never been to the Mocambo Club, but she had a book of matches in her handbag. Oh so that's what put him on to it. That's clever you know, very clever . . . Of course, the trail of footprints in the snow. All made with a size 10 left-footed shoe. So it had to be someone who could walk comfortably in two left shoes. That told him it was a small man who had put a big man's shoes on to lay the suspicion on somebody else. But he didn't realise that in his hurry he'd put two left shoes on. Well I never thought of that. I've been waiting for two one-legged twins to turn up.

Sid Come on, come on, so who done it then?

Tony He's coming to it, it's on the last page, I told you that. Here we are . . . *(Reads)* So, Inspector, you can see that the only person who could have done all these murders is the man sitting over there. So saying, Johnny Oxford pointed his finger at . . . *(He turns the page over to look at the last page. It isn't there)* Men are you skinny, do you have sand kicked in your face, if so . . . wait a minute, that's not right. *(Feverishly examines the pages)* There's a page missing. The last page is missing! *(He looks on the floor, then on the chair where he has been sitting)* Where's the last page? *(To Sid)* What have you done with the last page?

Sid I haven't touched it.

Tony *(looks again at the book)* Well, where is it? It's gone. The solution's on the last page. Oh, this is ridiculous. Here I am, a bag of tensed-up nerves waiting to see who did it, and this happens. It's enough to drive a man round the twist. I must find that last page.

Sid Show me the book. *(He examines it)* There you are.

Tony What?

Sid See that jagged edge along there . . . it's been torn out.

Tony Torn out?

Sid Yeah. They probably lit a fag with it or something.

Tony Lit a fag with it? The last page? They can't do that. There's plenty of other pages. This skinny bloke for a start, he could have gone without any hardship whatsoever. But the last page of a murder mystery. This is sheer unmitigated sadism.

Sid All right, what's done's done now. That's mystery in itself, isn't it? Who tore the last page out? I know who done it.

Tony Who? Who?

Sid The murderer, so nobody'll know who it was. *(Laughs.)*

Tony Very very funny. I must know who did it. I've got to find that last page.

Sid Forget about it. It's only a book. Read another one.

Tony Don't be such a fool. How can I read another one with that one still haunting me? *(He begins to pace up and down)* The last page of all pages. What a terrible nerve-wracking thing to do to a chap. The last page.

Fade on Tony pacing up and down.

Fade up the bedroom. Tony is in his dressing gown and pyjamas, Sid is in his bed trying to sleep. Tony carries on pacing up and down.

Tony The last page . . . fancy tearing out the last page. How could anybody do a thing like that.

Sid appears from under the bedclothes.

Sid Oi! Why don't you turn the light out and go to sleep.

Tony I want to know who did the murder.

Sid And I want to get some sleep. And if you don't turn out the light and stop pacing up and down, there'll be another murder they'll be trying to find out who did it. Now go to sleep.

Tony reluctantly gets into his bed and turns the light out. The room is now in darkness.

Tony *(after a pause)* You were the same when you couldn't think of the name of that bit player in 'Wagon Train' yesterday. You were up all night pacing up and down trying to think of it.

Sid *(muffled)* Go to sleep.

Tony I wonder who did it? *(Pause)* I know!

The light goes on and he is sitting upright in bed.

Tony I'll work it out for myself. I'll deduce it! I'll be Johnny Oxford. All the salient points are in the book, it's like a jigsaw puzzle . . . just fit it together and you've got the solution. You don't need the last page. *(Takes the book)* Let's see now . . .

Sid turns over and covers his head. He is furious. Tony takes paper and a pencil and a notepad from the table next to his bed.

Tony Now — list of characters in order of appearance. This is where my theatrical training comes in. Jocelyn Knockersbury . . . no, she was the first one who was done in. We'll cross her out. Johnny Oxford . . . no, he couldn't have done it. Let's see, how was Jocelyn done in? *(Refers to book)* Ah yes. Strangled with one of her own nylons. That means whoever did it had access to her stockings. Oh dear, I don't think I'd better pursue that line of enquiry. Freda Wolkinski was asleep in her pull-down bed, when somebody pressed the button, and she flew up into the wall and suffocated. That must have been somebody who knew her bed was a pull-down one . . therefore they must have been familiar with the topography of her boudoir. Therefore . . . Hmmm. I don't think I'll pursue that line of enquiry either. Still, no, no when you're a sleuth, you've got to be prepared to be confronted with the seamy side of life. After all, New York is probably a lot racier than East Cheam. I mustn't let my natural prudery detract me from the work in hand. Now . . . people associated with her — three girl friends, all murdered . . . two boy friends, one in the Navy in Japan, and one in California with an alibi. Now . . .

Sid's patience is exhausted. He jumps up in bed, and snatches the book from Tony's hand.

Sid Will you turn it in and go to sleep.

Tony Give me my book back. I want to find out who did it.

Sid Go to sleep.

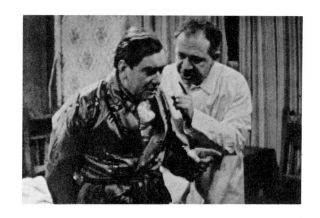

'. . . somebody who knew her bed was a pull-down one'

Tony I refuse to go to sleep until I have solved the mystery.

Sid Well, I'm not laying here all night listening to you rabbiting away to yourself. I'll tell you who done it.

Tony How?

Sid I'll skip through it and work it out. I know how they go about it. Don't forget, I've been involved in many a smart bit of detec-

tion. It shouldn't take very long to work out a load of rubbish like this. Then perhaps we can all get some kip.

Sid settles back to read the book. We see that the clock reads 12.25. Fade.

Fade up the bedroom again. The clock now reads 6.15. Sid is still in bed, now on the last knockings of the book. He reads the last page and puts it down.

Tony *(still awake)* Well, who did it?

Sid *(annoyed)* How do I know who did it? The last page is missing.

Tony Well I know the last page is missing. You said you'd tell me who did it.

Sid Well how did I know it was going to be so involved? I thought it was going to be a straightforward bash on the nut up a dark alley.

Sid lights a cigarette and starts smoking.

Tony Oh well, we'll just have to go to sleep.

Sid How can I go to sleep when I don't know who done it?

Tony No I know . . . it's so frustrating, isn't it.

Sid Let's try and sort it out between us.

They both get out of bed and start pacing up and down.

Sid Now then, who was the bird who drunk the carbolic milk shake?

Tony You mean the fat one.

Sid That's her. Now she's the key. Because she knew about all the others. So whoever did her in must be the murderer, and she must have known him and his relationship with the others.

Tony Yes, so if we can sort out who was nearest to her, we've got him.

Sid And that was the personal manager.

Tony Yes, of course. It was him. Harry . . . er . . . Harry . . .

Sid Belafonte.

Tony Not now Sid, no jokes. Harry . . . Zimmerman!

Sid That's him. Well that's that solved. Harry Zimmerman.

Tony Dear oh dear, thank goodness that's solved. I wouldn't have been able to think about anything else if we hadn't found it. *(Satisfied)* Yes, Harry Zimmerman.

They climb back into bed.

Sid Yes, perfect, he knew all their backgrounds, he knew where they were all living . . . he knew all their habits . . .

Tony Of course he did, and he had opportunities to do it, he could call round on the pretext of business . . . they wouldn't have suspected him. Oh yes, he's the only one who could have done it.

Sid Well that's a relief. He was little too, that explains the shoe theory . . .

Tony Yes, it all fits in. Well, well, Harry Zimmerman. Thank goodness for that. Now we can get some sleep. *(He pulls the curtains)* Thanks very much Sid. I don't know what I would have done if I hadn't found out. Harry Zimmerman . . . of course, it's obvious now, you've explained it. Oh well. *(Yawns)* Goodnight.

Sid Morning.

Tony Oh yes. *(Yawns again)* Good morning. Harry Zimmerman eh?

They sink beneath the bedclothes. Pause. Suddenly Tony sits bolt upright and throws the bedclothes off.

Tony Harry Zimmerman, he was killed in chapter three, you great buffoon! Why don't you read the book properly . . .

Fade on Tony's anger and Sid's puzzled expression.

Fade up the Library. The Librarian is at the counter. Tony and Sid stride in and up to the counter.

Tony I demand an explanation.

Librarian Now what?

Tony Where is the last page of *Lady Don't Fall Backwards*?

Librarian At the end of the book, surely.

Tony Oh well that's more like it I . . . it's not at the end of the book. Look. *(Shows him the book)* It has been torn out.

Librarian *(examining the book)* Did you do that?

Tony Oh for crying out . . . if I'd done it, would I have come in here and asked you where it was?

Librarian Well you did some very strange things in here yesterday.

Tony Have a care, good man. You can go too far you know.

Sid Let me deal with him. *(Threateningly)* Now listen mate . . . if you place any value on your teeth, you won't be so saucy. *(Shows him his fist)* Twenty-three knockouts in that. I could make it twenty-four — no trouble.

Tony You want to take notice, one wallop from that, you'll go right through the auto-biographies.

Sid Where's the last page?

Librarian I don't know.

Tony Well who did the murder then?

Librarian I don't know, I haven't read it.

Tony It's your book, you should know what they're all about. What sort of a librarian are you?

Librarian I can't read them all.

Tony *(inspired)* Wait a minute . . . another copy. Have you got another copy?

Librarian No, we only buy one of each.

Tony Oh this is ridiculous.

Sid goes over to the reading table. It is the same lot who were there the day before, in the same positions.

Sid Oi! . . . has anybody here read *Lady Don't Fall Backwards?*

Woman I beg your pardon?

Sid Have you read *Lady Don't Fall Back-wards?*

Woman I . . . I'm afraid I don't read books like that.

Sid Don't give me that jazz. You like a bit of spice the same as everybody else. Come on now . . . who done it?

Woman Who done . . . who did what?

Sid Who did the murders in *Lady Don't Fall Backwards?* You must have read it.

Woman I don't know what you're talking about. Please go away before I call the police.

She gets her smelling salts out and has a sniff.

Sid All right, all right, forget it. Go back to sleep.

Sid returns to the counter where Tony and the Librarian are still arguing.

Tony Are you sure you haven't got another copy?

Librarian I'm positive.

Tony Well what could have happened to the last page? You must see the book when it comes in.

Librarian Perhaps the previous reader knows something about it.

Tony Of course! That's it! Who had it out last?

Librarian I don't know.

Tony Well have a look then. Really, you're not being very helpful.

The Librarian looks in the book.

Librarian Er . . . here we are . . . last taken out, June 21st 1951.

Tony 1951. Must have been a best-seller, that one.

The Librarian refers to his file.

Librarian There was a threepenny fine, so we might have a record of the person who took it out.

Tony That's more like it. We're cooking with gas now, man.

Librarian Pardon?

Tony Johnny Oxford — in the book — that's what he says. I believe it's a phrase employed when one is being favourably impressed with the prowess of another chap.

Librarian I see. *(He gets a card out of his file)* Yes here we are — Proctor, W., Mr, The Larches, Oil Drum Lane.

Tony Oh yes, very salubrious. Thank you very much. I only hope he's still there.

Sid Oh do me a favour . . . it's nine years ago. He's forgotten all about it by now.

Tony It's a chance we've got to take.

They walk away, then Tony comes back.

Tony *(secretive)* I suppose *Lolita's* still out?

Librarian Yes.

Tony Oh.

He goes off again with Sid. Fade.

Fade up outside The Larches, a broken down Victorian house. Tony and Sid go up to the door. Tony knocks. The door is opened by a wild-eyed man.

Man What do you want?

Tony Mr Proctor, W.?

Man Yes.

Tony Oh good. We've come to see you about a book.

Man Book? What book?

Tony *Lady Don't Fall Backwards.*

The man's face lights up.

Man *Lady Don't Fall Backwards* by Darcy Sarto?

Tony That's the one. You remember it?

Man Of course I remember it. Have you read it?

Tony Yes, and . . .

Man *(grabs him)* Who did it? Who did it? I must know who did it. Who did it?

Tony Have you gone raving mad? I don't know who did it, that's why I'm here, I thought you might know.

Man How should I know, the last page was torn out.

Tony Oh cor. *(To Sid)* Come on, there's no point in staying here.

They turn to go.

Man *(frantic)* You can't just go like that. I spent six years trying to find out who did it . . . it's only these last three years I've managed to forget about it, now you come along and start it all up again.

Tony Yes well I'm very sorry, if we find out who did it, we'll come round and let you know.

Man *(grabbing Tony's coat)* No, no, you can't leave me like this. Where are you going?

Tony We're going to find the one who had it before you.

Man I tried him. He got fed up with it half-way through and never finished it.

Sid We'll go to the publishers then.

Man I went there six years ago. It's out of print, and they haven't got a single copy left.

Tony Well there must be a copy in a shop somewhere.

Man No, all the unsold copies went back to the publishers. They've been repulped. We'll never find out. *(Nearly breaks down)* Never. . . never.

Tony There, there, don't take on. Don't break now . . . not after all these years. Johnny Oxford wouldn't, would he? He wouldn't give up and break down.

Man No, no, that's true. He'd keep going wouldn't he? He'd find a copy wouldn't he?

Tony Of course he would. And so will we.

Sid Here . . . what about the original manuscript?

Man I never thought of thought of that.

Sid Who'd have that then?

Man The author.

Tony Darcy Sarto. Of course! And even if he hasn't got the manuscript, he'd remember who did it. Come on, let's find out where he lives. *(To Man)* Chin up, I think we're nearly at journey's end. *(He puts his hand on the man's shoulder)* As Johnny would tell you if he were here today . . . stay with it man.

Sid and Tony leave. Fade on the man drawing himself up, and keeping his feelings in check. His face is twitching with emotion.

Fade up the outside of a Georgian terraced house. Tony and Sid go up to the door.

Tony Here we are, 44. This is it Sid, at last we'll know. Straight from the horse's mouth. The author himself.

Tony rings the doorbell once, and then again.

Tony *(impatient)* Come on, come on.

He bends down and calls through the letter box.

Tony Come on, put that pen down. I know you're in there. Come along now please.

Sid *(taps him on the shoulder)* Hancock.

Tony brushes him off.

Tony I'm not giving up now. *(Into letter box)* Come on. This is disgusting. Come on. *(Bangs on door)* Open this door.

Sid *(taps him on the shoulder again)* You'll have a long wait.

Tony What?

Sid Look.

Sid indicates an L.C.C. plaque on the wall, which reads as follows: 'Darcy Sarto, novelist. lived here. Born 1884 died 1949.' Tony is completely floored.

Tony Dead. The fool. He can't do that to me. No consideration some people. How am I going to find out who did it now?

Sid Let's face it, we're not going to find out. Let's turn it in, I've got other things to do than go chasing round the country after dead authors.

Tony Never, I'm going to find out if it's the last thing I do. *(He has a sudden idea)* Wait a minute, of course.

Sid Now what?

Tony The British Museum!

Sid He won't be there, they've buried him I expect . . .

Tony No, no, not him, the book. The British Museum keeps a copy of every book that's published in this country. Why didn't I think of it before. All we've got to do is to go to the British Museum, borrow the copy, turn to the last page, and there. Cab . . .

They walk off picture, Tony waving his walking stick. Fade.

Fade up shot of the British Museum, dissolve to inside an office. Tony and Sid are waiting.

Tony You see, I told you so, they've got it. There's not a book published they haven't got.

The British Museum Librarian comes in holding a book.

Librarian I've found it. I think this is the one you're looking for.

He blows the dust off, and shows it to Tony.

Tony That's it. That's the one. *(Laughs triumphantly.)*

Librarian Not a very good copy I'm afraid. A very interesting binding though, they're using a new process of glueing the sheets to the . . .

Tony snatches it from him.

Tony Give us it here. I'm not interested in how they glue it. Oh these civil servants. It's not mutilated in any way?

Librarian No, no.

Tony It's all here?

Librarian Oh yes, yes of course.

Tony I can hardly look. *(Opens the book,*

then quickly shuts it) It's there! Page 201, it's there!

Sid Well come on, open it, read it out.

Tony Yes, of course. *(Opens the book at the penultimate page)* I'll give you three sentences in. So, Inspector, you can see that the only person who could have done these murders is the man sitting over there. So saying Johnny Oxford pointed his finger at . . . *(He turns the page over)* Men are you skinny, do you have sand kicked in your face, if so . . . where is it? *(Shakes the old man)* Where's the end? Where's the last page? What have you done with it?

Sid has picked up the book as Tony dropped it on the desk.

Sid The last page is here.

Tony is shattered.

Tony *(sits down weakly)* So nobody knows.

Librarian Is there any other book you would like to look at?

Tony No thank you. I've finished with books. I'll never read another book as long as I live. There ought to be a law against selling books with no ending. The Chinese had the right idea, start from the back and work your way forward, you wouldn't catch them like that.

Librarian It's not unusual. Edward Drew, Franz Kafka, they all had unfinished works published.

Tony Exactly. You never know what you're buying. Well I'm not going through all that

Tony *(Lets go of the old man)* Where? Where?

Sid There it is . . . there's a publisher's note on it. *(Reads)* At this point Mr Darcy Sarto's manuscript ends. He died before he could finish the story. We decided to publish it because we thought the countless Johnny Oxford fans throughout the world would like the opportunity of reading what there was of Mr Sarto's last work.

again. No more books for me. I shall take up some other art form. The gramophone perhaps. Yes, the gramophone. I'll go and buy one.

Fade and fade up the flat. He is just putting the finishing touches to placing one loudspeaker. There is another loudspeaker and a gramophone.

Tony Now, the chair must be eight feet from the loudspeaker. You've got to be just right with this stereophonic lark.

He lines up where the chair should be by pacing out eight feet, one foot in front of the other. He sits down.

Tony That's it. I mustn't break the triangle. Two hundred and fifty poundsworth of equipment here. All set up ready to blast myself out of my chair. *(Sings a bit)* Boom boom boom boom de-boom de-boom de-boom . . . Ha ha, that's it. This is better than whodunnits. No messing about. You know where you are with this stuff. Two hundred and fifty quid. All I need now is a gramophone record. Where's Sid got to? It doesn't take this long to buy a record. If he's been down the Hand and Racquet with my last two pounds . . . I'll . . . I'll . . .

Sid comes in with a gramophone record wrapped up in a paper bag.

Sid Yeah, I couldn't get you Beethoven's Fifth. I thought you might like this instead.

Sid hands him the record. Tony takes it out of the cover, puts the cover on the table. He looks at the label on the record.

Tony Very funny. Very, very funny. Schubert's Unfinished Symphony.

Tony quite deliberately breaks the record over Sid's head and walks off.

We see a close up of the record cover on table. Fade on the screen filled by the cover reading 'Schubert's Unfinished Symphony'.

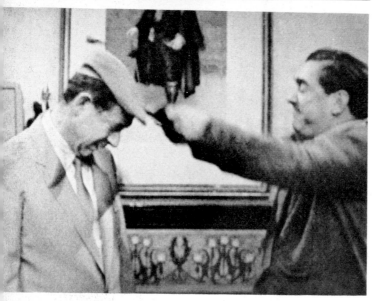

THE REUNION PARTY

'My goodness me, there's more water out there than there is in your beer'

The inside of an off-licence. Tony comes in carrying a bag full of empties, walks to the counter and sets it down.

Tony Evening Harry.

Harry Evening Mr H. Nice weather for the ducks, eh?

Tony You're right there. My goodness me, there's more water out there than there is in your beer.

They both laugh good-naturedly.

Harry Very cold for this time of the year, isn't it?

Tony Oh, perishing. Absolutely perishing.

Harry What's the forecast then?

Tony More to come. I've just been watching the bloke on the television. Sticking little metal clouds all over the place he was. The trouble is, as he was saying, there's a deep depression sitting over Ireland you see . . . It's moving in, by tomorrow midday it'll be covering the whole of southeast England, southern Ireland, and the Home Counties. *(Pause, then confidentially)* South Cones have been hoisted.

Harry They haven't.

Tony They have.

Harry *(pause)* What are they?

Tony I don't know . . . but they've hoisted them. It's gale force seven up at Finisterre.

Harry Get away.

Tony No straight up. Reaching gale force nine by tomorrow morning. Of course it's the fishermen I feel sorry for.

Harry Yes, me too.

Tony I wouldn't have their job for a hundred quid a week. Stuck up there in those little boats with South Cones hoisted all around you. And we moan about the price of herrings, eh? *(Laughs.)*

Tony moves his bag of empties along the counter so that it is between himself and the barman.

Tony Well, there we are. How much on that little lot, then?

Harry starts taking the bottles out of the bag and looking at them.

Harry Well that's not mine for a start. *(Moves the bottle to one side)* Neither is that one . . .

Tony How do you know, how do you know? I took the label . . . I mean there's no label on it.

Harry I know, but you left a bit round the stopper. Look — Ellermans and Hunters. We're a Groynley House, we don't sell these. Don't try and come the old acid with me, boy. I know too much about the game. Wine bottles, nothing on those . . . nothing on spirits . . .

He takes the last bottle from the bag and puts it on the counter.

Harry Here we are. That's fourpence. What do you want, a packet of crisps?

Tony No, I'll have three arrowroot biscuits. Fourpence on this . . . It's absolutely disgusting. I've a good mind not to give you my order. It's a big one.

Harry What, *two* miniatures this week?

Tony *(pause)* You're a bit sarky tonight, aren't you? What's the matter with you, somebody knocked your pile of pennies over? Pin

your ears back. This'll probably clear you right out. Now then — *(He refers to his list)* I want ten crates of stout, winter brew . . . five crates of best brown . . . twelve quarts of Dragon's Breath . . . two barrels of bitter . . . two crates of Danish lager . . . and a barrel of rough cider.

Harry Cor blimey, are you going to have a party?

Tony No my grandmother's coming over . . . of course I'm having a party. Now — three bottles of Harkers Gin, six bottles of whisky, two bottles of rum, Pirate's Pleasure. Right, that's it then. I want it delivered for tomorrow night, please.

Harry Cor blimey, this is going to be a right booze up, isn't it? You won't get through that lot, surely.

Tony What? This is just to get the dust out of their throats. We'll be back tomorrow night for the main order.

Harry Who's coming to this party, then?

Tony I'm having a little reunion of my old Army pals. The Third East Cheam Light Horse. Three of the heaviest drinkers who ever set foot inside a pair of army boots. Do you know, I haven't seen them for fifteen years.

Harry Get away.

Tony No, fifteen years. You mark my words, Harry, there'll be some high jinks down the Cuttings tomorrow night. You won't be able to hear the trains going by. By heavens, these blokes can't half put it away. You should have seen our demob party. Drinking it by the bowler hatful we were. Ah, it'll be just like old times. Well, this isn't going to get the baby washed, is it Harry?

Harry Goodnight Mr H. I'll send the boy round with the stuff in the morning.

Tony goes to the door and opens it. Another man comes in.

Tony Evening. Cor, dear oh dear, look at it.

Harry Still raining, is it?

Tony Pelting down it is. Takes the curl right out of my astrakhan collar, this weather. I think it's that bomb, you know. It's upset the ionosphere. We never had weather like this when I was a kid. Oh well. *(He pulls up his collar)* Here we go . . . over the top . . . splash, splash.

Harry Don't do anything I wouldn't do!

Tony *(laughs)* I won't. Oh well, olive oil — as the earwig said as he fell off the wall . . . here we go.

Tony leaves, and the other man walks towards the bar.

Man Who was that?

Harry One of my customers.

Man Cor dear, you get them all in here, don't you?

Harry Yeah. Well, how are you Fred? Nice weather for ducks, eh?

Man You've said it there. Oh dearie me, there's more water out there than there is in your beer. *(He laughs.)*

Fade on the barman casting an exasperated glance towards the ceiling.

Fade up Tony's flat. On the mantelpiece there is a picture of Tony in uniform, saluting, with a Union Jack either side of the frame. Tony walks over to the mantelpiece and salutes his picture. There are two tables in the middle of the sitting room, cloth-covered, on which all the bottles are arranged. Also in evidence are glasses, plates of sandwiches, etc. Sid comes in carrying a crate of beer.

Sid There you are, that's the last one. *(Puts it down)* Thirsty work, that is.

'Oh well, olive oil – as the earwig
said as he fell off the wall . . .
here we go'

He takes a glass and picks up a bottle of beer.
Tony slaps his hand away.

Tony Get your hands off. You weren't a member of our regiment. If you want some beer hold your own reunion. The King's Own Glasshouse Deserters, weren't they?

Sid Reunion, me? I should cocoa. What do I want to meet any of that mob again for? I can't understand you . . . this morbid desire to cling on to the past.

Tony It's not a question of clinging on to the past. It was the wonderful feeling we had in those days. A bunch of young chaps, thrown together from all walks of life, were joined together with a sense of purpose, mutual respect, and bound by a deep everlasting friendship that time will never erase.

Sid Well I don't know what sort of regiment you were in, mate, but it wasn't like that in mine. As soon as the shells started coming over we disintegrated. First bloke on the motor bike was off, never mind about the others.

Tony Well it wasn't like that with us. It was one for all and all for one. Beautiful friendships were formed in those days, born in the heat of battle, and forged in the plonk bars of Cairo. Ah, you'll love them Sid, they're a marvellous bunch of lads. The four of us, like quads we were . . . Smudger Smith, Ginger Johnson, Chalky White, and me.

Sid Kippers Hancock.

Tony How did you know they called me Kippers?

Sid With your feet what else could they call you?

Tony The condition of my feet in those days was quite different to what they are today. Chasing the Hun across Europe, that was what flattened these, mate. I collected these feet trying to make Britain a better place to live in, so don't let's have so much of it.

Sid Blimey, don't be so sensitive. It was only a little joke.

Tony Well I don't like little jokes about my feet. As far as I'm concerned my feet represent a war wound.

Sid All right, I'm sorry.

Tony All right then. If I'd been an American I would have got the Purple Heart for these. Probably two, one for each plate. Smudger, Ginger, and Chalky never used to laugh about my feet. They were true friends. The Four Musketeers we were called. Inseparable we were. Wherever they went, I went. Did I ever tell you about that time in Benghazi . . .

Sid Hundreds of times.

Tony When Smudger got the chicken out of the cookhouse . . .

Sid Yes, I know.

Tony And he stuck it up his blouse and ran away . . .

Sid Yes, I know all about it.

Tony And another officer shouted out, 'Who's that running away with a chicken stuffed up his blouse?' . . .

Sid That's the one, yes, you told me.

Tony And old Smudger yelled out, 'Hancock!' Oh dear, oh dear, I'll never forget that . . . Laugh?

Sid You were courtmartialled for that, weren't you?

Tony Yes. *(Pause, then bitter)* He was a card. He was always doing things like that. You couldn't help liking him. I must have done about two years for him . . . on and off. And women. Could he get the women. He was the only man I knew who came back from Dunkirk with two women.

Sid Two of them?

Tony Well it's too far for one to row, isn't it? Yes, yes, he was a lad. Up against old Smudger, Errol Flynn's confessions look like the ramblings of a backward choirboy.

Sid Well of course, we had blokes like him in our mob . . .

Tony No, no, not like him, I'm sorry. I'm trying to impress upon you, we were different. Did I ever tell you about the time we got drunk in Naples?

Sid Everybody got drunk in Naples.

Tony Not like we got drunk. Roaring stiff we were. We couldn't stand up. Up to here in Chianti we were. Standing on top of Vesuvius pouring in bottles of vino redo. Nearly put it out. It was just the same in battle, too. Tough.

'Did I ever tell you about the time we got drunk in Naples?'

'Which way's Berlin? . . .
. . . Right that's
the way we're going'

Tough? Savage is more the word. *(He growls)* There we were, dug in just outside Anzio, when the order came through — retreat on all fronts. I looked at Smudger, just like I'm looking at you today, and I said, 'Which way's Berlin?' He said, 'That way.' *(Points)* I said, 'Right, that's the way we're going.' So we were off. Me, Smudger, Ginger, and Chalky. Well when the Germans realised we meant business they threw everything at us. They brought up their eighty-eight millimetres. Well that did it. We assembled our twenty-five pounders. Twenty-five pounders against eighty-eight millimetres. The only chance we had was to try and shoot their shells down before they landed. Or better

still, put one down the barrel of their guns and hit their shell just as it was coming out, thus putting them out of action. So we moved forward. And then what do you think? Old Smudger had forgotten the shells. There was only one thing for it . . . hand grenades. We pulled the pin out with our teeth *(he mimes this)* . . . rushed forward . . . chickety snitch. . . and threw them *(brings arm over as if throwing one).* What an explosion . . . right on their ammo dump. I've still got a piece of metal inside me.

Sid   You have.

. . . 'right on their ammo dump. I've still got a piece of metal inside me'

41

Tony Yes, I swallowed the pin. *(Pats his stomach)* It's still there. I can always tell when it's going to rain.

Sid It's a pity you didn't swallow the hand grenade. What a load of old codswallop.

Tony Well you wait till you meet them. You'll see what sort of men they were. Heroes, mate.

Sid Well, we had heroes in our mob too.

Tony Not like these, Sid. We were the bull-dog breed. Kipling stuff we were.

Sid Yes, well I remember once we were dug in outside Florence when . . .

Tony It wasn't the same Sid, we were specially trained.

Sid So were we.

Tony Not like we were.

Sid Well we used to get up to some things too . . .

Tony No, not like we did Sid.

Sid I remember one occasion, we were advancing on Tripoli, and all of a sudden our tanks stopped . . .

Tony A similar thing happened to me. I was . . .

Sid And just because I'd been had up before for flogging petrol to the Arabs, they all looked at me . . .

Tony So we were waiting to make this parachute jump and we thought it would be a laugh if we all four of us jumped on the same parachute, you see . . .

Sid So I said, 'It's no use arguing, Rommel will be diggin' in,' so we rounded up a couple of camels and off we went after him . . .

Tony So we dropped three thousand feet, clinging on to each other's ankles, and suddenly I said, 'It's about time somebody opened the parachute.' We looked up and half the panels were missing — old Smudger's girl friend had had a go at it . . .

Sid So there we were, two on each hump, covered with sand . . .

Tony So we dropped like stones, saw a jeep going down past us on six parachutes, so we jumped in it, started the engine and as soon as we hit the ground we were off. Well, the Germans put down their rifles and applauded. They said 'We can't fight against this sort of thing . . . ' You were saying something?

Sid Nothing, nothing. I can't fight against that sort of thing either. Do you mind if I have one of these pastry things with the minced-up bird stuffed down them?

Tony I take it you are referring to the chicken *vol au vent?* No you can't, I'm saving those for Smudger. He's always hungry.

Sid I get hungry as well.

Tony Not like he does. He's a quick thinker, too. Did I ever tell you about the time in Germany when he was absent without leave and the red caps finally caught up with him in a house with a German bird, and he said 'Thank goodness you've arrived, she's been holding me prisoner for three months.' And he got away with it . . . Oh there'll be so much to talk about. All those old days, eh? This is going to be a party the like of which they've never seen around these parts.

There is a knock on the front door. Tony jumps up and looks at his watch.

Tony It's them, they've arrived. Sid, they're here! *(He puts a medal on his jacket, and smartens himself up)* Stand by for the avalanche. You won't know what hit you — they'll go through this house like a tornado. When the four of us get together all hell will break loose.

Sid Yeah all right. I'll go and let them in.

Sid leaves the room to answer the door. Tony claps his hands together and walks about excitedly.

Tony This is going to be another do like that last night in Rome.

Sid returns to the sitting room.

Sid *(announcing)* Mr Smudger Smith.

'Smudger' walks in nervously. He is dressed in a bowler hat, raincoat, and scarf. Tony goes forward to greet him, his arms open.

Tony Smudger, Smudger . . . Smudger?

Smudger How do you do?

Tony *(incredulous)* How do you do? Chickety snitch!

Smudger Pardon?

Tony The old greeting. You haven't forgotten? Chickety snitch — remember?

He goes through an exaggerated mime of pulling a pin out of a hand grenade and throwing it.

Tony Then as my hand came over you grabbed it, over your shoulder, I'd do a double flip . . .

He claps him on the shoulder and punches him playfully in the midriff. Smudger coughs, and doubles over, as the blow hurts him.

Tony What's the matter?

Smudger Tummy trouble. It's nothing much.

Tony Oh don't worry about that, I've got something for that. The old favourite, eh?

He goes to the table and takes a bottle of whisky and a large glass.

Tony Eh? How much, the usual? Right up to the top . . .*(He begins to pour the whisky)* Say 'when' when it's running down the side of the glass, eh?

Smudger Er . . . no thank you, not for me.

Tony *(stunned)* Pardon?

Smudger No, I don't take it these days. *(Pats his stomach)* The tummy, you know.

Tony Yes, but this is a celebration. Fifteen years . . . come on, what are you going to have? Come on, we've got the lot here, anything you like.

Smudger Well . . . I'll have a small sherry.

Tony Sherry? We haven't got any sherry.

Smudger Oh well, I won't bother then. If you'll make me a cup of tea I'll have one.

Tony A cup of tea? *(With sudden realisation)* I know. Don't tell me . . . the Cairo special? With a dollop of rum, eh?

Smudger No, no, no, just milk and sugar, thank you.

Sid Well don't just stand there, get a cup of tea for the avalanche.

Tony Oh I'm terribly sorry, I'm forgetting my manners. This is Mr Sidney James, Mr Smudger Smith, my old comrade in arms. And may I say it, Smudger *(he puts his arm around him)*, my best friend.

Smudger Don't call me Smudger.

Tony Don't call you Smudger . . . that's your name, isn't it? You haven't got another name, have you?

Smudger Yes. Clarence.

Sid reacts.

Smudger I don't want the name Smudger to get round, it might jeopardise my position at the bank. I've got my own window now, you know.

Tony *(composing himself)* Oh good. I always said you'd get on. What happened to the plans you had for when you got out — whale fishing, and lumberjacking, and crocodile hunting in Australia?

Smudger Well, I thought it over and I decided the security at the bank was a better idea.

Tony But what about that restless urge for adventure you always had? Surely a job like that can't satisfy a firebrand like you.

Smudger Oh well, it's quite exciting. Sometimes at the end of the day we're five shillings short — it's quite thrilling.

Tony Oh yes, I can see that. *(With renewed gaiety)* Well come on, take your hat and coat off. Make yourself at home. Here we are.

Smudger takes off his hat and coat to give to Tony, but keeps his scarf.

Smudger I'll hang on to the scarf . . . I might catch cold.

Tony Er, quite. Ah, it's been a long time, Smudge . . . er . . . Clarence.

Smudger Yes.

Tony We've got a lot to talk about, about the old days.

Smudger Yes.

Tony Here, I know what I wanted to ask you. What ever became of that ATS girl you were

knocking about with? You know the one, big hooter, the one you used to take out for a bet, she's got great big feet. Oh she was a shocker . . . you remember. What ever happened to her?

Smudger *(coldly)* I married her.

Tony Oh. Well yes, I remember her now, nice girl she was, er . . . nice disposition she had, yes I er . . . get me a drink Sid. Have one yourself. Beauty's only skin deep.

Smudger Actually, I wanted to ask you a favour. Er, Mavis — my wife — she doesn't like me going out on my own, so I took the liberty of asking her along. I hope you don't mind.

Tony Well I er . . . well . . .

Smudger I never go out without her.

Tony Oh well, in that case . . .

There is a knock on the door.

Smudger That'll be her now. She dropped off at the chemist to get my medicine. I'll go, don't you bother. *(He leaves.)*

Sid So that's the Errol Flynn of the East Cheam Light Horse. I'm glad the others are coming. Be a nice hysterical exciting evening with him and his missus. I'll turn the television on.

Sid starts to get up but Tony restrains him.

Tony You'll do no such thing. And keep your voice down.

Sid Why, he's probably hard of hearing as well, poor old devil.

Tony He's not a poor old devil, it's fifteen years, he's shy, that's all. We haven't met for such a long time. You wait till the evening goes on, I'll bring him out a bit. You'll see what a laugh he is. Ssh . . . say nothing. *(Louder)* So I said to Val Parnell, either my name goes above the juggler, or I don't appear so we . . . oh, there you are.

Smudger and Mavis have walked into the room. Mavis is a very severe woman.

Tony *(rising)* Mavis . . . as beautiful as ever. You haven't changed a bit. *(He walks towards her, arms out)* How about a kiss for your husband's best friend, eh?

Mavis I'd rather not, you never know what these things lead to.

Tony Yes, yes . . . well. Come on, sit down. Have a drink. Come on, we've got to get rid of all this tonight. What are you going to have, then?

Mavis I don't drink.

Tony No, I didn't think you would.

Mavis Drink is the refreshment of the devil.

Tony Yes, well, I hadn't looked at it quite like that. It's a point of view, I suppose, a valid one . . . I admire you for your, um, strength . . . I couldn't do it myse . . . Have a cigarette.

Mavis I don't smoke.

Tony Oh.

Tony offers the box to Smudger, who reaches for one.

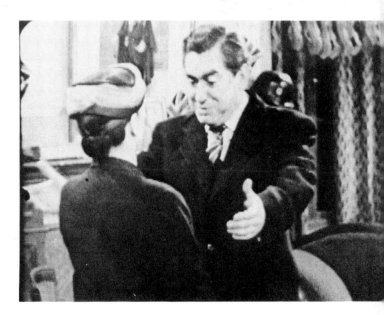

Mavis   And neither does he.

Smudger   No . . . *(Sitting back again)* I've given it up.

Tony   Well . . . I'll sit down then. A lot to talk about, isn't there, about the old times . . . eh?

Smudger and Mavis are sitting bolt upright on the edge of their chairs.

Tony   *(smiles)* Well . . . this is nice . . . Been looking forward to this. Seeing you again after all these years, Smudger.

Mavis   Clarence.

Tony   Yes. Yes, of course. Clarence. You and your good lady wife here . . . *(Pause)* Ah, how the memories come flooding back, don't they, hey? Remember about that time in Tripoli? *(Starts to laugh)* When the four of us went down to that bird's house and her father came

out and . . . no I think we'd better forget about that.

Pause. Tony and Sid fidget. Smudger and Mavis stare straight ahead. Tony smiles at them.

Tony   Well, this is nice. *(Starts to laugh again)* Here, I've remembered somebody now. This'll bring it all back to you. Remember Dopey Kent?

Smudger   No.

Tony   Yes you do, of course you do. Tall bloke, a corporal from Bradford, we all took the mickey out of him 'cause he had funny teeth. *(He does a rabbit)* You remember him.

Smudger   No, I can't place him.

Tony   Yes of course you can. He was going about with that posh NAAFI girl from

Walthamstow — you remember. We nailed his boots to the ground one day and blew reveille . . . he was in hospital for three months. You remember him.

Smudger No.

Tony *(implacable)* Yes, you do. He was in the next bed to that fat fellow with the funny hair, now what was his name.

Smudger Warner?

Tony No, no. Um . . . Post . . . no, no, it wasn't him.

Smudger *(pause)* Ryman?

Tony No, no. *(Pause)* Got a head like a sieve. Little fat fellow — got stuck in the turret of his tank that time when the ammunition started exploding and we all laughed. What was his name?

Tony spends some time trying to remember the man's name, hitting his head with his hand etc. Several times he seems to have it just on the tip of his tongue, only to lose it again. Finally he gives up.

Tony Um, well anyway, he was in the next bed to this other fellow.

Smudger What other fellow?

Tony The one with the funny teeth. We all . . . *(Despairingly)* Oh, what's it matter.

Pause. Tony hums a bit. Sid looks at his finger nails. Smudger and Mavis just stare in front of them.

Tony Well, it's been a long time.

Smudger Yes. Certainly has.

. . . 'he had funny teeth. You remember him. . . . now what was his name?'

Tony Yes, it certainly has. Been a long time. Fifteen years. Yes, that's a long time all right.

Smudger Yes, a long time.

Tony Yes.

Another pause, punctuated by a few throat clearings. Sid stretches.

Mavis *(to Clarence)* We mustn't leave it too late, dear.

Shot of Tony's reaction, a cor blimey one. Pause. Tony starts to play with his fingers, smiling at Mavis and Smudger. They are all dead bored.

Tony Here.

Smudger Pardon?

Tony Guess who's coming tonight.

Smudger Who?

Tony *(triumphantly confident)* Ginger Johnson and Chalky White.

Smudger who?

Tony Oh, for crying out loud. Ginger Johnson and Chalky White! We were never out out of each other's sight . . . the Four Musketeers.

Smudger Oh, I think I can remember. How are they?

Tony How should I know, I haven't seen them for fifteen years. Dear oh dear, the things we used to get up to. *(To Sid)* You'll like Ginger, he's a bundle of laughs.

Sid *(sourly)* Yeah? I could do with one.

Tony You'll like him. He's right up your street. *(To Mavis)* You'll like him as well — life and soul of the party. Honestly the things he used to do — stands on his head he does and drinks a pint of beer without spilling a drop, and when he puts a woman's hat on he's a scream, he's got Mae West off to a tee, he used to get these two balloons and he . . . *(Mavis is staring at him coldly)* . . . he . . .

Tony gets up quickly, takes a plate of sandwiches, and walks over to Mavis.

Tony How about food? You do eat food, I take it?

Mavis No thank you, I don't eat the bread of today. We make our own.

Tony Well take the bread off and eat the meat.

Mavis I'm a vegetarian.

Tony offers the plate to Smudger.

Smudger Er . . . no . . . I . . .

Tony The tummy, I suppose.

Smudger Mavis has got a nut cutlet waiting for me at home.

Tony Oh good heavens man, you're not a squirrel. Have a sandwich.

Mavis Mr Hancock, there's no need to make fun of other people's beliefs. If we choose not to eat meat, nor to drink alcohol, that is our affair.

Tony It's all right for you. I've gone to great expense to get all this booze down here, not to mention food . . . what's going to happen to all that? Stone me, he used to nosh like nobody's business in the Army, and what a boozer he was, the Chianti used to be up to here, and women . . .

Mavis That's quite enough. We wish you wouldn't keep talking about when he was in the Army. The past is past, and Clarence doesn't wish to be reminded of his more foolish days. Do you, dear?

Smudger No, dear.

Tony I don't know why you bothered to come.

Mavis Well if that's how you feel about it . . . *(They start to get up)* Come, Clarence.

Tony No, no. Sit down. I'm sorry . . . *(Tries to laugh.)*

Sid Oh, let them go. I've had more fun at a funeral.

Mavis I don't think we need any of your rudeness, Mr Whateveryournameis. Don't you think that your sarcastic looks and mutterings have gone unnoticed. Or the way you've been sitting over there — drinking rather heavily, to my mind.

Sid *(gets up and walks towards Mavis)* Look here, girl. You may be able to push old avalanche around, but don't you start on me . . .

Smudger Don't you speak to my wife like that.

Sid Wait a minute, mate. You may have been a bit of a tearaway fifteen years ago, but I don't go a bundle on your chances now.

Tony Now, Sid, please . . .

Sid You keep out of this. This is the most exciting part of the evening up to now. As I was saying, if you wouldn't mind stepping outside, I'd be only too willing to oblige with a mouthful of knuckles.

Tony No, Sid, please. No bounce ups at my reunion. Sit down, have a drink. *(To Smudger and Mavis)* Don't go. Wait till Ginger gets here, you'll like him, he's a card. *(There is a knock at the door)* That'll be him now, that'll be Ginger, now we'll get things going. All friendly and lively, just like the old days, eh? Ha ha . . . he's a million laughs this boy. Go and let him in, Sid. Keep your hands occupied . . .

Sid leaves to answer the door.

Tony *(to Mavis)* Take no notice of Sid, he's got a heart of gold really. It was the war. He blows up now and then, like we all do. Sit back and enjoy yourself . . . Ginger will liven things up.

Sid comes back to the sitting room.

Sid Mr Ginger Johnson

Ginger enters. He is also a meek little man, wearing a flat cap and a raincoat.

Tony *(approaching, arms out)* Ginger, it isn't . . . isn't . . . it can't be . . . It is — Ginger.

Ginger takes his hat off. He is bald.

Tony Good old . . . where's your hair? You had a great mop of flaming red hair.

Ginger Well, it's been a long time. None of us are getting any younger, are we, Smudger?

Tony That's true, I . . . I'm not Smudger! I'm Hancock.

Ginger Are you? *(He puts on a pair of glasses)* Oh, yeah . . . so it is. How's your feet?

Tony *(to Sid)* See, I told you he was a laugh.

Ginger *(sees Sid)* Hallo, Chalky, I haven't seen you for a long time.

Sid The name's Sid . . . Chalky hasn't turned up yet.

Tony Here, come over here. Before we get down to the serious drinking, while you can still focus . . . turn around. Look who's here.

Ginger *(turning)* Stone the crows, Dopey Kent.

Tony *(angry)* It's Smudger! It's Smudger . . . the Four Musketeers.

Ginger Oh, of course, Smudger.

Smudger Clarence. How do you do?

Ginger and Smudger shake hands.

Ginger Well, well, well . . . Here, whatever happened to that ATS girl you were roaming about with? You know, the one with the big hooter.

Tony Come away . . . I told you he was a million laughs. What a joker. He pretended he'd forgotten you . . . *(Laughing)* Dear oh dear. Great thing, friendship. We can all rib each other without being insulted.

Smudger and Mavis regard Tony stonily.

Tony What about a drink, Ginger? You always had the biggest capacity of all of us. What are you going to have?

Ginger I'll have a small sherry.

Tony *(angry)* We haven't got any sherry.

Ginger Oh it doesn't matter. It doesn't worry me whether I have any or not.

Tony Well, it worries me. I've got to get rid of all this lot. Sixty-eight quidsworth here. This is supposed to be a celebration. Fifteen years. What's wrong with you lot, what's happened to you?

Sid Look, why don't we put the telly on and have a little nap.

Smudger That's a good idea. I am feeling a little washed out.

Tony Oh, shut up. What a farce. Ginger, put a woman's hat on or something. Leap about a bit. Give us your impression of Mae West. I've told them all about it.

Ginger. Me? That wasn't me, that was Dusty Miller.

Tony Oh, cor . . . *(Offers the plate)* Have a sandwich.

Ginger No, I've just eaten, thank you.

Tony slings the plate on the table in disgust. They sit down.

Pause.

Sid I bet you lot have got lots to talk about.

Ginger Yes, yes. Oh yes. Fifteen years. It's a long time.

Smudger Yes, a long time. A lot of water's flowed under the bridge since then.

Ginger It certainly has. Yes, it's a long time.

Smudger Yes, it certainly is.

Pause.

Ginger *(looking around)* Nice little place you've got here.

Tony Somewhere to live.

Ginger You're something to do with show business these days, aren't you?

Tony stares ahead coldly. Sid laughs.

Ginger Who got you into that? You never struck me as being very funny in the old days. Still, I suppose you're no worse than some of them who are on. Dear oh dear, what a load of old rubbish.

Mavis nudges Smudger and points to her watch. Smudger indicates that they will go in a minute. There is another pause, with a few yawns, etc.

Tony Chalky's late, isn't he?

Sid *(handing a scrapbook to Tony)* Here, why don't you pass this round? It might sort of re-capture some of the magic.

Tony *(interested again)* Oh yes, I forgot this. Ah, there's some memories in here. Here's

one . . . the four of us sitting in a jeep outside Reggio with the Italian hats on. *(Gets up and takes the scrapbook over to Mavis and Smudger)* This'll make you laugh. Just your sense of humour.

Mavis *(coldly)* Who's that woman?

Tony Oh . . . just some peasant girl, grateful for being liberated. You had some better ones of her, didn't you Smudger, with that camera you pinched. They did the rounds those pictures, didn't they, eh? Eh? Ha ha . . . do you remember that one of her where she was . . .

Smudger has a fit of coughing.

Tony What's the matter? Have I said something . . . oh. *(To Mavis)* No, it was a mistake. It wasn't him, it was Ginger.

Ginger It wasn't me.

Tony Well it was me then. What does it matter? Forget all about it . . . there's loads of other pictures there. I cherish those.

Smudger, Mavis, and Ginger are all completely disinterested.

Tony Every picture a story . . . a link with the past.

Tony shuts the book and puts it down.

Ginger *(unenthusiastically)* Yes. Very interesting.

Tony Have you got yours, then?

Ginger I shouldn't think so. I didn't bother.

Tony *(to Smudger)* Have you got yours?

Smudger *(quickly)* No, no, no, no. Nothing like that. I've got one of me in uniform the day I got married.

He offers it to Tony.

Tony *(disinterested)* It's like you. *(Shows it to Sid)* Clarence in uniform the day he got married.

Sid *(hardly looks at it before passing it on to Ginger and back to Tony)* Charming. Very sexy.

Ginger *(to Tony)* You never took the plunge then?

Tony No, not me. I value my own freedom too much for that. I saw what it did to some of the lads I used to know. Ruined them . . . *(He realises Mavis is annoyed)* Well, I mean it suited some. I shall probably do it myself you know, when Miss Right comes along . . . ha, ha . . . er . . .

Pause.

Mavis Well I think we ought to be going, Clarence.

Tony No, no don't go. Chalky isn't here yet. You must meet Chalky. Actually he was the real live wire amongst us. He was the one who really was behind all the things we used to get up to. The capers he used to think up. Without him we were quite dull — hard to believe, I know. A bundle of energy he was, and he knew more stories than any man in the Army. Where he got them from I do not know. Risky they were, yes, but never coarse. He used to have us in fits. Oh wait till he gets here. It'll be just like old times.

There is a knock on the door.

Tony Here he is! The man we've been waiting for. I bet he's got some more stories. Sid, go and let the ringleader in. Fifteen years . . . he'll have us up all night.

Sid leaves.

Tony I laugh just to think of him. Honestly the stories he used to tell . . .

Sid comes back.

Sid Mr Chalky White.

Chalky enters, smiling broadly. He is wearing a trilby, overcoat, and scarf.

Chalky Hallo Tony old son.

Tony Chalky. Chalky White as I live and breathe. *(They pump each other's hands)* You haven't changed a bit. Tell us some of the old stories . . . you know, some of the ones you used to tell in the barracks room. Take your hat and coat off. Get the booze out, he'll sink that lot in half an hour. Course we've all heard them, but it's the way he tells them. No one can tell the one about the British officer in the girl's flat like he can. Come on now, Chalky, let's hear that one.

'Get the booze out, he'll sink that lot in half an hour'

Chalky has taken off his coat. He removes his scarf and we see that he is a Vicar. Tony hasn't noticed this, having turned round to the others. He now turns back to the Vicar.

Tony Come on Chalky, what are you waiting for . . . liven the place up. Don't tell me you've

changed as well, I . . . *(He sees the collar)* Oh cor, he has.

Fade on Tony, completely disillusioned. Fade up the hallway. The guests are just leaving. Tony and Sid are seeing them out.

Tony Cheerio, Smudger, it's been a very successful evening. *(Bitter)* Just like the old days . . .

Smudger We must do it again.

Tony Yes, about 1975 . . . at your place. *(Hands Mavis a bottle of beer)* Here you are, have a bottle of beer, you can wash your hair in it. Goodnight. Cheerio Ginger, it's been most enjoyable. We'll make a regular do of this, eh?

Ginger Well . . . I don't think we'll bother, do you?

Tony No, perhaps you're right. Well, look after yourself.

Ginger And you. *(Puts up his collar)* Hallo, it's raining again. Nice weather for the ducks.

Tony I think it's the bomb.

Ginger Yes, I expect you're right. Well, goodnight.

Tony Goodnight. Well, cheerio Chalky . . . er . . . your Grace . . . er Vic . . .

Chalky It's been perfectly splendid meeting you again.

Tony Well, best of luck in your new job.

Chalky *(puts his hand on Tony's shoulder)* Peace be with you my son.

Tony Yes. Thank you very much, you're too kind.

Chalky follows the others out the door. Tony waves them goodbye, then closes the door.

Tony What a farce. I've never seen three men change like that in all my life.

Sid Well what did you expect? Fifteen years, that's a long time in anybody's life. People change. I bet they're thinking right now how you've changed, and how pathetic you are.

Tony I am not pathetic.

Sid I told you it was a mistake in the first place. Never try and recapture the past.

Tony Perhaps you're right Sid. I suppose one should be content with one's memories.

Sid Come on, let's get drunk. Let's see who can drink the most without taking the bottle out of their mouth.

Tony Yes, all right.

There is a knock on the door.

Tony Hello, one of them must have forgotten something.

Tony opens the door, to find a man standing there, full of life. The man comes in, slapping Tony jovially and repeatedly on the shoulder as he speaks.

Man Hallo, hallo, hallo, Tony boy. I'm here and raring to go. Remember me, Scrounger Harris? Well come on, let's get at the old beer, then, eh? Boy have we got a lot to talk about . . . The old greeting, eh? Chickety snitch . . .

The man begins to go through the hand grenade routine. Tony slams the door in his face just as the man's hand finishes the arc.

Tony Hoppit. *(To Sid)* I remember him, the most miserable perisher in the whole regiment. *(They each take a bottle of beer)* I'll give you a toast. To absent friends, and long may they stay that way. Good health!

Fade on Tony and Sid drinking their toast.

HANCOCK ALONE

Open with an aerial view of the Earl's Court area of London. We see a long street with Victorian terraced houses either side. Close up of one building, then of the dozen or so name plates and bells by the door, ending on the top one which says 'A. Hancock'.

Dissolve into Tony's room, which is a typical bedsitter. A single bed is up against one wall. There are a few pin-ups on the wall, coloured photos of sumptuous feasts from American magazines. Odd bits of furniture are scattered about the room, including a table, a gas fire and meter, a wardrobe with a full-length mirror on the door. There is a television set on

another puff, then gives up. After a moment's pause, he sings a bit of Noel Coward —

Tony   A room with a view, and you . . .

He stops suddenly and lies silent for a few moments, then yawns. He looks around the room slowly. His feet catch his attention. He wiggles them, then puts one foot vertically with the heel resting on the bed. Then he puts the other foot on top of it with the heel resting on the toes. He takes the bottom foot out and places it on top of the other one with the heel again resting on the toes. He takes the

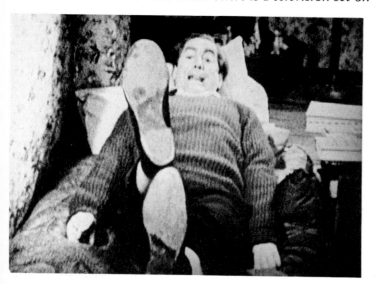

a table in one corner with a record player on top of it and a small radio on top of that. Some books are opened face downwards on the table — Das Capital, The Outsider, Look Back in Anger, The Decline of the West, The Intellectual in a Decadent Society, Glam (a magazine with a pin-up on the front), The Prisoner.

Tony is lying full length on the bed, which is made. He is fully dressed, staring up at the ceiling, smoking a cigarette. As he is lying there he starts trying to blow smoke rings. He contorts his face as he blows the smoke out, but he doesn't succeed. He takes another puff and this time taps his cheek with his finger as the smoke comes out, but this doesn't work either. He takes another draw and tries again, but the same thing happens. He takes still

other one from underneath and repeats the operation. Now his two feet are a couple of feet off the bed, one on top of the other, and causing a strain on his stomach muscles. These give way and his feet collapse on the bed. He rubs his stomach muscles and winces.

Tony   Getting old.

He takes another puff on his cigarette, which is now quite short. Puffs again, this time holding the cigarette between his thumb and forefinger with the rest of his hand cupped round it. He squints his eyes a bit and speaks out of the free corner of his mouth.

Tony   So I says to this geezer . . .

He winces as he burns his lip.

Tony I burnt my lip!

He gets up, gingerly holding his lip. He walks across the room to his small kitchen, which is just off the main room. There is a cabinet above the sink, and he opens it and looks at the various bottles of medicine, ointments, pills, etc. All the bottles are old, with the white stuff resting on the bottom and the brown stuff on the top. He takes one of the bottles and looks at the label.

ones. Who gave them to me? That Indian doctor. What was his name? Peter Sellers. *(Laughs)* No it wasn't. It was a good film though. *(Resumes his search)* Oh, a nose dropper. I own a nose dropper. Nothing to put in it but I own a nose dropper. *(He turns to face the room, holding the dropper in the air)* Extra! Extra! Read all about it . . . *(Turning back to the cabinet)* Oh there's nothing here. I must have a clear out, one of these days.

He slams the cabinet door shut and sticks his lower lip out. He has a look at his burn in a hand mirror.

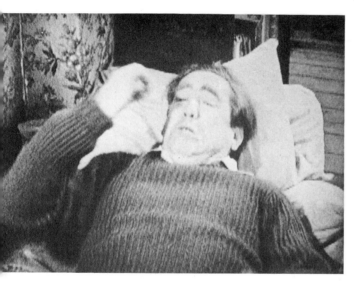 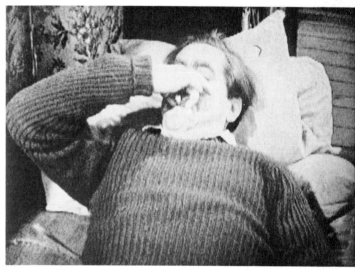

Tony What have we got here then? *(Reads)* Master A. Hancock, Lower 4B. That's a bit old, isn't it? *(He shakes the bottle, takes the cork out and sniffs it. He nearly passes out)* Cor, dear oh dear. *(Puts the cork back in)* That was pre-National Health, I know. Where are we? There must be something here. *(He rummages around in the cabinet)* There's enough stuff here to keep Emergency Ward 10 going for a fortnight. I shall have to have a clear out. Oh me night-light. Oh good, I've been looking for that. *(He puts it on one side)* Ointment, ointment, ointment. Ah . . . *(Takes a round cardboard box and opens it)* Pills. If I was looking for pills I'd have nothing but ointment. Just my luck. *(He takes a pill out)* Blue and yellow, what are they for? *(Has a think)* My allergy? No, those are the blue and white

Tony I must put something on it. I might get lockjaw. I know. Butter. *(To the mirror)* A touch of the old New Zealand.

With his lip still sticking out, he goes over to the larder. He takes the butter dish out, and puts some on his lip. Now he can't put his lip back or he'll lick the butter off. He walks back into the main room with his lip sticking out, passes the big mirror on the wardrobe, stops, and looks at himself. He begins to sing, impersonating Maurice Chevalier.

Tony Every leetle breeze seems to murmur Louise. Birds in the trees seem to twitter Louise. *(Talks)* Just to see and hear you gives joy I never knew . . .

He forgets the rest of it and just makes French sounding noises, then shrugs and gives up. He peers into the mirror to see what effect the butter is having on his lip.

Tony Hallo, I've licked the butter off. *(Runs his tongue along his lips)* Still, it's better than zinc ointment. I wonder if the milkman's been yet. I haven't heard him. Only I'd like a cup of tea. *(To his reflection)* That's what I would like, a cup of tea. A — cup — of — teeeeee.

At the end of this sentence his lips are stretched out full, revealing most of his teeth. He turns his head to the side.

Tony Hello, Brough. *(Turns his head back the other way)* Hello, Archie.

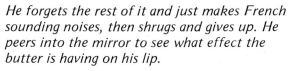

Turning his head back and forth and nodding like a ventriloquist's dummy, and with his teeth still showing, he carries on a dialogue between himself and Archie Andrews. At the end of this he finds he is looking at himself in the mirror.

Tony *(still as Archie)* I'll have to stop smoking.

He fingers one of his front teeth.

Tony *(own voice)* Is that loose . . . or is it my fingers going in and out? I'll have to get that seen to. *(He preens in the mirror)* Not a bad set of choppers really. There's a good few bites left in them. All your girl friends have said that. 'Tone,' they've said, 'Tone, you've

got a good set of teeth.' They've all said that. *(He runs his finger along the upper row)* Yes, there's no sugar decay there, mate. *(Pause)* I wonder which one's the bicuspid. I've been wanting to know that for years. *(He tries out the word to savour the sound of it)* Bicuspid. It's a funny word, that is *Bi*cuspid. Bi*cus*pid. Bicus*pid.* By cuspid he's a handsome devil, Sir George.

He laughs and moves away from the mirror. Mimes taking a pinch of snuff, and then does a little dance and bow. Then he stops, and raises his arms, cupping his hands round the back of his head.

Tony Bicuspid. I suppose it's Latin. Bi, meaning two. One on each side. Cus . . . cus

meaning to swear. Pid . . . meaning pid. Greek probably. Yeah, pid — Greek for teeth, I should think. That's it then. Bicuspid. Two swearing teeth. I suppose so. I bet I'm not far out anyway.

He goes to the bed and flops down on it. Sighs. Pause.

Tony What was I doing before I burnt my lip? Blowing smoke rings. No, before that. What was I lying on the bed for in the first place? Reading . . . of course. *(He looks a-round for his book, finds it, and opens it)* I'd better finish it, it's due back tomorrow. Where was I . . . oh yes, chapter 24. Three to go.

He starts reading. After a while he looks puzzled.

'Hello, Brough.
Hello, Archie'

Tony I don't remember him. Arthur Whitaker? What happened in the last chapter?

He turns back to the last chapter. Mumbles to himself as he reads and skips through the chapter.

Tony I don't remember any of this. What happened before then? Oh, she'd met him and they'd gone up into the hayloft together. I remember that bit. Very good. *(He smiles in pleasure as he remembers it)* I must read that bit again. And before that he . . . no, no, it's gone. Oh, it's a waste of time me reading. I can never remember what's happened.

through the dictionary, looking for another word. Finds it.

Tony Well if that's what they mean why don't they say so? *(He reads again for a few words)* Oh, I don't know what he's talking about. The Limit and Scope of Human Knowledge. Well we've soon found out my limit, haven't we? Three sentences. No, no, I should know. It's in English, I should know what he's talking about. He's a human being, same as me, using words, English words, available to us all. Now, concentrate.

He puts the book away and lies back.

Tony Too much going on in my mind, you see. Nuclear disarmament, the future of mankind, China, Spurs, oh it's very hard to be an intellectual these days. Let's have a go at old Bertie Russell. *(He takes one of the books off the table, and settles back on the bed)* Now then, let's have a good look at this. *Human Knowledge — It's Limit and Scope.* By Bertrand Russell. Introduction.

He reads a couple of sentences, then looks puzzled. He reaches for a big dictionary on the table at the side of the bed, and thumbs through it. He goes back to Bertrand Russell, sees how the word's meaning fits in, and looks pleased. Reads another few words. Thumbs

He starts reading again. The meaning begins to dawn on him, but then he loses it. He does business trying to fathom it out, nearly getting there, but falling back into complete incomprehension. He starts to reach for the dictionary but changes his mind.

Tony No, it's him. It's him that's at fault. He's a rotten writer. A good writer should be able to put down his thoughts clearly, in the simplest terms, understandable to everybody. It's him. He's a bad writer. I'm not going to waste my time reading him.

He tosses the book away, and picks up another one. We see that it is Lady Don't Fall Backwards.

Tony   Ah, that's more like it.

He opens it and starts to read. He gets a few sentences in, then looks up puzzled. He turns towards the dictionary on the table, then throws the novel down.

Tony   I'm not going to strain my eyes any more.

He makes a few noises, then gets up. As he is walking across the room he suddenly breaks into a small sprint, as if bowling at cricket.

Tony   *(Australian)* Here's Richie Benaud, bowling from the pavilion end. He comes down . . . *(Stops abruptly)* Oh dear.

He looks around for something to do. Spies a chocolate box, which he picks up and shakes – there is one chocolate in it. He opens the box, takes out the chocolate and compares it with the plan on the box.

Tony   *(disgusted)* Marzipan! *(He tosses it back into the box)* Oh dear, oh dear.

He wanders over to the window and stares out, glumly. Fade on a view of his face through the window, and then fade up the same shot.

The telephone rings. He dashes over to it, diverted at last, and feverishly picks up the receiver.

**'Leopardskin tights
and a green
sweater. Yes, lovely'**

Tony Hallo, Earl's Court 3972. Yes. Who? Fred? Fred who? There's no Fred here. Yes, 3972. Ah, wait a minute . . . yes, I think I know. Yes, he must have been the gentleman who had the room before me. Did you try the landlady? *(Smiles)* Yes, she is, isn't she? Fancy him not telling you where he's gone. *(He takes the phone over to the bed and sits down)* A nice young lady like you. No, no, no, no. I mean, you sound very nice. I don't know who you are . . . Joyce? Joyce. *(He relaxes and lounges on the bed, playing with the telephone cord as he talks)* A nice name, I like that. Anthony. Oooh, you know, sort of . . . well built. No, not fat. Well built I said. Tallish. No, not quite six foot. Taller than average though. Why don't you er . . . come round and see?

(He chuckles confidently, then sits up worried) No, no don't misunderstand me. I'm very sorry, no, you sound a very nice girl. I'm sorry. That's better. *(Chuckles and relaxes again)* Yeah. Work? Well . . . it just so happens that I don't agree with the social system as it is. I've contracted out, I just sit here and contemplate. Who's a beatnik? I don't see eye to eye with the establishment on the . . . no, I haven't got a beard. A party? Well, you'll just have to go with somebody else, won't you? Who, me? No, no, no, no. I'm not doing anything, no, no, no, no. No, I can read my books tomorrow. Don't worry about the books, I like parties, I'd love to go really . . . please. Gin and cider party. Yes. I'll bring a bottle. No, cider. Shall I pick you up, then? Oh, how

**'. . . smart?
Flapping about on
the tow path
at Richmond'**

will I recognise you? Leopardskin tights and a green sweater. Yes, lovely. What time? Eight. Till tonight then. Bye.

He puts down the phone, and claps his hands.

Tony Whoo, whoooo! Ha, ha, ha, ha! *(Gets up)* I think I turned that round nicely. *(Looks into mirror)* Oh, you devil. Crafty. *Crafty.* This is only the beginning. As soon as I get in with that mob, there'll be loads of birds there, that's for sure. And they'll all be lonely. Bedsitter land. There's no holds barred round here, it's just a question of waiting, and . . . I . . . shall . . . be . . . *in,* mate! I won't be stuck in here many more nights. *(He looks at his watch)* Let's see now. Half past four. *(Feels his face)* Better not shave yet, it might start coming through again. I think a couple of hours with Bertie is called for. *(He goes over and sits on the bed)* Yes, I've got time for half a dozen chapters, I shouldn't be surprised. Leopardskin tights and a green sweater . . . oh dear me.

He begins to sing and opens his Bertrand

Russell book to the first page of chapter one. We see that the clock near his bed says 4.30 p.m. Fade.

Fade up on the clock, now reading 7.00 p.m. Tony is still on the bed with his book, and we see that he is still on the first page of chapter one. He closes the book, looking puzzled.

Tony Well, well, well, isn't that remarkable. A man of eighty-eight, writing this. It's amazing. I'll just about have finished it by the time I'm eighty-eight. Oh well, seven o'clock, first things first. Time the peacock showed his feathers, I fancy.

He gets up and walks over to his wardrobe. Opens the door.

Tony Now, what are we going to wear tonight? What goes with leopardskin tights? I wish I'd bought those suede trousers now. What a sensation they would have been. Mind you, they're all right when you're standing still, a bit stiff if you want to move about though.

'Razor blades – for men'

'You've never had it so good. The winds of change . . .'

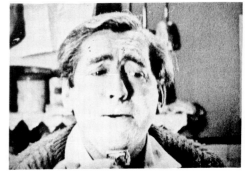

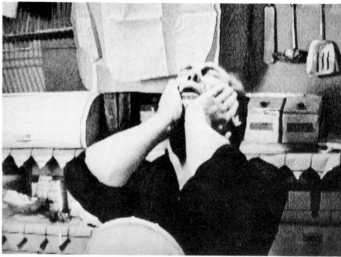

He rummages about in the wardrobe and takes out a pair of trousers which are hanging on a coat hanger. They have great wide bottoms.

Tony Well, I haven't got time to have those taken in. How did I ever think they were smart? Flapping about on the the tow path at Richmond. Looking like something off of H.M.S. Vanguard.

He takes out a pair of jeans with big six inch turn-ups.

Tony Ah, that's more like it. Very racy. There's nothing like a nice tight pair of jeans to get them going, eh? Nice tight jeans. See the legs right the way up. And why not? If you've got good legs, why not show it? *(He*

turns so he can see his legs in the mirror and gives a little kick) Dancer's legs those are.

He takes the trousers he is wearing by the crease and pulls them tight so his calf is outlined under the material. He smacks his calf.

Tony Look at that. Solid. Not an ounce of flab there. That's what cycling does for you. If you want to get a leg, get a bike! *(Pause)* To go with this I think we'll have the black open neck shirt and the medallion. Harry Belafonte . . . *(He swings the medallion round)* If she looks half as good in her leopardskins as I will in this lot, she'd better watch herself, that's all I can say.

'Oh, it'll drive her berserk, this will'

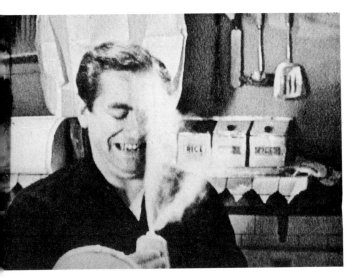

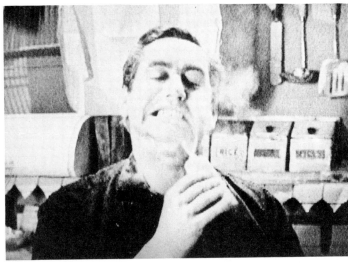

He dances about the room in high spirits, singing to himself — 'We are in love with you, my heart and I . . .'. Still singing, he goes into the kitchen. Takes his shaving mug from a shelf and fills it. He places a hand mirror in position so he can see what he's doing, then takes his razor in one hand and brush in the other.

Tony Oh you can't beat the cold steel and the badger. All this electric rubbish, wheels spinning round all over the place . . . For callow youths and peach fluff . . . but not for a man's beard. *(Deep voice)* Razor blades — for men.

He has been lathering the brush during this. He now lathers his top lip, so he has a white moustache. He looks at the effect.

Tony *(as MacMillan)* You've never had it so good. The winds of change . . . *(He lathers the rest of his face)* I think we'll have this on nine. *(He adjusts the razor accordingly, then looks up)* If you're going to have a shave, have a close one.

He prepares himself for the ordeal, and then makes a stroke on his chin. He winces, and then begins shaving his cheek. Fade on him shaving.

Fade up on Tony still in the kitchen, now clean-shaven. He is buttoning up his black shirt.

Tony That's that for three days. Now then, some of the old after-shave lotion.

71

... 'something I want
to listen to anyway.
... A talk on
Etruscan vases'

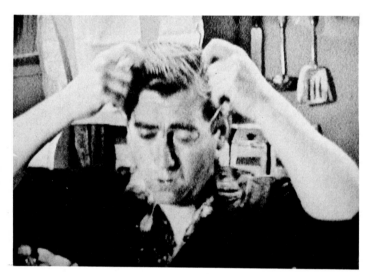 

He takes a bottle of astringent and shakes some on to his hand. He knows this is going to burn like mad and hesitates to do it. He steels himself, then applies it. It does burn, and he yelps at it. He holds his face and jumps about, then finally recovers.

Tony Why I put that stuff on I do not know. Fancy paying good money for something that hurts you. *(Pats his face)* It doesn't even smell very much anyway. I think we ought to give her the lot.

He takes out a couple of tins of talcum powder from the cabinet, and holds one in each hand.

Tony What shall we hit her with? The Attar of Roses, or the *(deepens voice)* Prince William ... for men. Prince William I fancy.

He sprays some talc on his face in a great cloud. He coughs, and wipes away the surplus. Then he carries on spraying more of the talc.

Tony Oh, it'll drive her berserk, this will. Stops them dead in their tracks at twenty-five yards this stuff. *(He brushes the excess powder off his shirt, leaving bits of it here and there)* Where's me medallion? Here it is. *(Puts it on, and starts singing)* Oh island in the sun ... went to bed with his trousers on ... noooo . . . . .

'Leopardskin tights at her age. How revolting'

'Eve has proffered the apple and Adam has slung it straight back at her'

The telephone rings and he rushes out into the main room to answer it.

Tony *(lazy posh)* Hallo, 3927. Yes, yes, yes. *(He picks up the phone, walks over to the bed, and starts to lie down)* Joyce. I'm getting ready. *(Sits up)* Cancelled? What do you mean, cancelled, I've spent hours getting read . . . Well that's nice, you might have told me. What about you, where are you going? Perhaps we could . . . oh, you've found Fred. Yes, well I hope you have a nice time. Oh, don't worry about me. I prefer being on me own, I'm just not a gregarious person, that's all. Gregarious. Oh. Hang on a minute. *(He stands up and looks through the dictionary, then walks over to the table with the telephone)* Yes, gregarious. Fond of company, to herd together. No, don't worry about me, there's something on the Third Programme I want to listen to anyway. (He brushes the remaining powder off his shirt) A talk on Etruscan vases. (Gay) Yes, all right, some other time then. (He slams the phone down) Stupid women! Why do they phone in the first place? Why don't they leave you alone? Leopardskin tights at her age. How revolting. She sounds a right crone. That was a lucky escape, I nearly got sucked into a social whirlpool there . . . diverted from my lofty ideals into a life of debauchery. The fleshpots of West London

have been cheated of another victim. Eve has proffered the apple and Adam has slung it straight back at her. That'll make a good play. I'll start on that in the morning. I'll tear up the one about the coloured student in Stoke Poges. That wasn't getting anywhere anyway. *(He sits down on the bed)* I feel strangely cleansed. Yes, I must watch myself a bit, I'm getting too easily diverted. Time is the most precious commodity at our disposal, I must not waste it. To waste one second of one's life is a betrayal of one's self. *(Pause)* I wonder what's on television.

He gets up and goes over to the table and picks up a newspaper.

Tony   There's only a Western again. Oh well, I'll put it on and get the set warmed up.

He goes over and switches the set on. Comes back to the table, and looks at the paper.

Tony   Tightrope or Bronowski, that is the question. I should watch Bronowski really. What was that he was saying last week? If I was a thousand light years away, my son would be fifty-four, I would be thirty-five . . . no, thirty-two . . . and my father would be ten and a half . . . in ratio . . . if I could get back in time. No, he must be up the spout there. He's all right on theories, but when it comes to adding up the sums, he's right out of his depth.

The set is now warmed up and we can hear the American voices of the Western. Tony looks at the television and sees that the screen is covered with lines, waving occasionally

Tony Oh — here we go again. Oh dear, oh dear.

He goes over to the set and fiddles with the knobs, but the picture stays the same. He bangs the set — no change. He begins to manipulate the antennae on the indoor aerial which is perched on the radio on top of the television, pushing and pulling them in and out, together and singly. This doesn't work either, and he starts to turn the aerial round in all directions. As he walks behind the set while doing this the picture becomes clear, but then goes back to lines again as he returns to the front. He picks up the aerial and starts moving about the room with it, pulling the antennae in and out. The picture varies in appearance but no image appears. He stands on a chair with the aerial and holds it above his head, then in his hands, then sticks his leg out and loops the aerial underneath it. There is still no image on the screen.

He gets down and walks over to the wardrobe. He opens the door and steps into the wardrobe, backwards, still holding the aerial. The screen begins to clear as he does this, and the picture is excellent by the time he is all the way in. He closes the door on himself, keeping his head outside and craning round to see the set.

Tony Oh it's hopeless. I can't stand here all day.

He gets out of the wardrobe, and the picture immediately returns to horizontal lines as at the beginning. He goes over to the television set and fences a bit with the aerial in front of it. This does no good, so he backs away over towards the window, watching the screen all the time. He opens the window and holds the aerial outside, but the picture stays the same. He clambers out of the window and sits on the sill with his legs inside. The picture gets a little better. He shuts the window down on his knees and the picture immediately gets quite good. He presses his nose against the glass and watches through the window for a while, then gets fed up, opens the window, and comes back into the room. As he does so the picture goes back to horizontal lines.

Still holding the aerial, he walks over to his front door and opens it. As he backs out into the landing the picture becomes increasingly better. He sets the aerial down on the landing and peers around the door into the room — the picture is now very clear. Leaving the aerial on the landing, he begins to creep back into the room. The picture is perfect as he tiptoes across the room, his eyes on the set. At one point the picture begins to go and he pauses in his tracks, swaying a bit on the spot until the picture becomes clear again. He continues to the table, and carefully pulls out a chair. He sits down and the picture immediately goes back to horizontal lines. Just as Tony realises what has happened, an announcer's voice replaces the background sound of the Western.

Announcer We regret this interference with your picture. It is due to circumstances beyond our control. We are doing everything we can to put it right. Meanwhile, here is some music.

With a maniacal laugh, Tony gets up and takes hold of the aerial cable. He pulls hard on it and the aerial comes sliding in through the door. Once it's in he stalks over to the set and switches it off. He starts rolling the cable round the aerial as he talks.

Tony I don't want to watch it anyway. I'll send it back in the morning. I'll get another one when they've got some decent programmes on.

Finished with the aerial, he sighs and presses the palms of his hands against his eyes.

Tony I think I'd better turn it in. Me eyes, like little needles they are.

He walks over to his bedside table, picks up a cigarette, lights it, and inhales deeply.

Tony I've got another big day tomorrow. Have me teeth seen to . . . and me eyes. *(Settles down on the bed)* It's all go, isn't it? Not enough hours left in the day, that's the

'I've got another big day tomorrow'

trouble. *(Sighs)* I think we'll have another go at Bert. See how we get on with him. *(He picks up his Bertrand Russell book and begins to open it)* No, I'll read it tomorrow.

He puts the book back on the table and settles back on the bed with his cigarette. Fade on Tony tapping his cheek with his finger in an attempt to blow a smoke ring.

THE BOWMANS

The scene opens on the inside of a radio studio, showing a sign reading 'On the Air'. The production staff are sitting in the control box, behind a plate-glass window. We hear linking music, and the producer signals the cast to begin the next scene. The cast members of the programme are grouped around a microphone in the studio, and they all have scripts in their hands. At the signal from the producer, the announcer steps forward to the mike.

Announcer Meanwhile, back at Brook Farm, Dan Bowman has his troubles too.

Dan Bowman Well those blasted crows have certainly taken all the seed out of this field, George.

George Ah, you're right there, gaffer. If we don't get a decent crop out of this field we won't have any winter feeding for the cows.

Dan Bowman That's true. Oh this farming life. If it's not one thing, it's another.

George Ah, yes.

Dan Bowman Well, it's no good standing here complaining about it, there's work to be done.

Mrs Bowman *(off mike)* Dan, I've brought your sandwiches and your flask.

Dan Bowman Hallo love, you think of everything, don't you. Here, you've been crying. What's up love?

Mrs Bowman   Oh it's nothing Dan.

Dan Bowman   Now come on, love, out with it. Something's upset you. You can't keep things from me. Come on, what's wrong lass?

Mrs Bowman   Well, it's young Diane. Mrs W. saw her coming out of the country club last night with Paul Black.

Dan Bowman   Paul Black. His divorce isn't through yet. Are you sure it was our Diane?

Mrs Bowman   Well, Mrs W. said she saw her.

Dan Bowman   He's no good, Gladys. Where does he get his money from? That's what I'd like to know. I don't like it, Gladys. Oh no, I can't believe our Diane would go out with the likes of him.

Tony, sitting against the studio wall and following the programme in his script, assumes an expression which says that he knows better about Dan Bowman's daughter.

Dan Bowman   There's plenty of decent lads in the village. I can't believe it.

Mrs Bowman   Well it's true Dan. Joshua saw her as well.

Dan Bowman   That old scallywag, you can't believe anything he says.

Tony, still seated, reacts with mock outrage.

Mrs Bowman   Well here he comes now with his dog. You can ask him yourself.

George   Over here, Joshua.

Tony walks on mike, dressed for the part in a battered old hat, old coat, corduroys with a strap above the knees, and a knobby stick under his arms.

Tony *(singing, with Suffolk accent)* I've got mangel wurzels in my garden, I've got mangel wurzels in my shed . . . I've got mangel wurzels in my bathroom, and a mangel wurzel for a head.

The rest of the cast is puzzled by this, and look at their scripts. The actor who plays the dog comes on mike yapping and snarling.

Tony Down boy, get down, down. *(The dog yaps again)* Get down, back you black-hearted creature, get down. *(The dog snarls ferociously)* Get down afore I fetches my stick across you. *(Tony and the actor are ready to have a go at each other)* Go on, lie down there.

The producer waves frantically at Tony. Tony points to the dog and mouths 'It's him'.

George Hallo Joshua, you old rascal.

Tony Hallo George, me old pal, me old beauty, me old darling.

Dan Bowman Joshua, I want a word with you.

Tony Well dang my breeches, if you don't all a-look all worried like. *(Dog snarls)* Get down, be quiet. *(Threatens the actor with a back-hander)* What be the trouble then, Dan me old pal me old beauty? Has the blight been at your turnips again?

Dan Bowman No, it's not that Joshua.

Tony Ah, then it's the kale up in North Meadow, it's gone to seed. I told 'ee to get it in last week, didn't I, but you wouldn't listen to old Joshua, no — no one listens to old Joshua. But he knows, old Joshua, he knows. *(The dog snarls and yelps)* I'm warning you. *(Prods the actor with his stick)* One more yap out of you and you get this down your throat.

Tony prods the actor again, hurting him this time, and the actor pushes Tony. Tony is just going to wallop him with the stick, when Dan Bowman signals them to stop it, and Gladys nudges Dan with her elbow to get on with it. He looks at his script to find the place.

Dan Bowman Er . . . yes . . . er, no it's not the kale either, I got that in during the spell of fine weather last weekend.

Tony Good, good, I'm glad to hear that Dan me old pal me old beauty. Then what be a-bothering you then?

Dan Bowman It's my daughter Diane.

Tony Ah, then you've heard about that no good city slicker Paul Black.

Dan Bowman Then it's true.

Tony Aaah, of course it be true. I've a been a-seeing of them with my own eyes. Coming out of the Turks Head they was. A-giggling and a-cuddling and a-kissing . . .

Mrs Bowman Oh Dan.

Dan Bowman Steady, love.

Tony Ah . . . but that baint be the worst of it.

Dan Bowman What happened Joshua?

Tony I'm a-going to tell you what happened. I'm a-going to tell you what I saw with me own eyes.

Mrs Bowman What did you see Joshua?

Tony I'm a-going to tell you what I saw.

Dan Bowman Well come on, out with it man. What did you see?

Mrs Bowman Yes, Joshua. What did you see our daughter and this man get up to?

Tony All right then . . . I'll tell you.

The signature tune of the programme begins — something similar to 'The Archers'.

Announcer You have been listening to 'The Bowmans', an everyday story of simple people. The News and Radio Newsreel follow in a few moments.

The producer indicates that they are off the air, and the actors relax. They turn on Tony.

Dan Bowman *(actor's own voice)* What on earth do you think you're playing at? Are you trying to ruin the programme?

Tony It wasn't my fault. It was him, the dog, barking where he wasn't supposed to. He was trying to drown me. I know what he's up to.

Actor I did not. I barked where I was supposed to bark.

Tony You did not. It's got down here three yelps and a growl. You were a-barking and a-snarling all over the place. I've never seen such a disgraceful exhibition of drunkenness in the whole of my professional career.

Mrs Bowman *(in her real, very educated, voice)* Well you shouldn't have poked him with that stick.

Tony Would you kindly keep out of this, madam? I am the oldest member of the community. Let's have a little respect.

Mrs Bowman You may be the oldest member of the village, Mr Hancock, but you are not the oldest member of this cast. Dan and I . . . Mr Osmington and I were the two originals. You were brought in after, and you can be taken out.

Tony What do you mean by that? I've been in this show for five years, I get more fan mail than all the rest of you put together. Twenty million people gather round their radio sets at a quarter to seven every night, just waiting to have a giggle at the antics old Joshua gets up to. I carry this programme. It's only me and my bits of homespun philosophy, and my jokes, and my little rhymes, that's what keeps them glued to the set, mate, that's what they're waiting for. Not you moaning all round the house about the weather and your daughter and your rock cakes. Say nothing — here comes the producer.

The producer has left the control room and comes into the studio.

Tony Hallo Ronnie, another good'un, eh?

Producer It was not a good one. You practically ruined the whole of the last five minutes.

Tony Who, me?

Producer You were putting bits in all over the place, and what do you mean by coming on singing that stupid song about mangel wurzels? That wasn't in the script.

Tony I know it wasn't. I made it up.

Producer You have no right to put bits in.

Omnes Quite right. Yes.

Tony I portray the character as I see him. That's the sort of song he would sing. And I thought as he'd just emerged from the Turks Head, it seemed quite reasonable to assume he would be singing. It's him who messed it up. Fido here.

Actor How dare you! I may tell you that I'm one of the finest dog impersonators in the country.

Tony You are supposed to be my obedient dog, you're supposed to do as you're told. Instead of that you yap around me feet all the time I'm talking. I'll get the scriptwriter to have you gored by a bull or something, get an alsatian in. Oh, I'm surrounded by amateurs.

There is an uproar from the other actors.

Producer All right, all right, stop quarrelling. Now, here you are, here are the scripts for Monday evening.

He hands a script to each of the cast, and they begin to look through them.

Tony Ah yes, we'll find out what old Joshua saw outside the Turks Head. (*He reads the first page, laughs*) Oooh, oh dear oh dear.

Fancy that. This is your daughter for you. Very good. (*He flips through the script*) What's this? Joshua falls in the threshing machine?

Producer Oh yes, I've been meaning to have a word with you about that.

Tony I should think so too.

Producer He falls in the machine and is rushed off to hospital.

Tony Oh. I see. A nice touch of human interest. Yes, old Joshua in hospital, what a good idea. I've got it — I'm on the danger list . . . hovering between life and death. Twenty million people crying their eyes out, slowly he pulls through, courageous old Joshua, jokes with the doctors, his first day up, chasing the nurses round the ward, until six months later he emerges triumphant from the hospital, stronger than ever.

Producer Well, not exactly. He dies on Tuesday night.

Tony He dies?

Producer Without regaining consciousness.

Tony Have you gone raving mad? You seriously imagine the public are going to stand for this? You'll have a howling mob outside Broadcasting House hurling bricks through the windows.

Producer I'm sorry, the decision has been taken. We're killing you off on Tuesday night.

Tony But you can't kill off the most popular character in the whole programme. It's ridiculous. If you want to economise why don't you put him to sleep (*indicates the dog actor*)?

Actor You can't get rid of me. I'm not just a dog, I'm the whole farmyard.

The actor does a quick medley of animal impressions.

Producer Yes, all right Harold, we're not getting rid of you. I'm sorry Mr Hancock, it's not a question of economy. Our audience research has found that the character of Joshua is falling off alarmingly in popularity.

Tony Oh this is nonsense. I've never been so popular. Look at last year when I proposed to Mrs W. and she turned me down. I had three hundred and thirty-two proposals of marriage in the next post. And when I had that cough — fourteen gallons of lung syrup turned up. I am a real person to the listening public, I'm one of the family, they'll go berserk if I snuff it.

Dan Bowman I doubt that very much. Miss Beaumont and I are the mainstay of this programme.

Tony Well I'm not standing for this. I'm going straight to the top.

Producer My instructions have come from the top.

Tony Oh. Well it's the scriptwriters. They don't know what they're doing. They've made me far too unsympathetic. Last week I kicked the dog three times.

Producer That wasn't in the script.

Tony Well no. But he asked for it, shoving in yaps where there weren't any.

Producer Yes that's another thing, your acting.

Tony And what is wrong with my acting?

Producer You're erratic. We never know from show to show what sort of performance to expect.

Tony Really. Don't you think these things, if to be said at all, should be said in the privacy of your office, and not in front of this crowd of gaping village idiots?

Producer You asked for this. People have begun to notice your accent.

Tony My accent is perfect. I spent six months in Somerset on a cider farm perfecting it.

Producer It's never the same two performances running. Sometimes it's Somerset, sometimes it's Suffolk, a bit of Welsh, Birmingham, and last week I could swear we had a bit of Robert Newton in there. It's just not good enough. It completely destroys the illusion we are trying to build up. Who can believe in a character who indulges in these . . . these vocal gymnastics?

Tony Vocal gymnastics. You're going too far, sir.

Producer And these ridiculous clothes you wear. This is a radio show.

Tony I wear these clothes to get the feeling of the part. Of course if you're completely ignorant of the Stanislavsky school of acting, I'm obviously wasting my time with this load of tat.

Producer We don't want method actors in here.

Tony I'm not a method actor. I don't just rush around the studio scratching myself. What do you know about it anyway? You come in here, an ex-sound mixer from Sports Report, telling me about acting. This is very nefarious, my good man. I warn you, if this is not put right over the weekend, I shan't be here on Monday for the *coup de grâce*.

Producer We've though of that possibility. We have an alternative script ready. So you can either go now and die over the weekend, or come in on Monday and get an extra day's pay.

Tony *(thinks about it)* I see. That's the way things are shaping, is it? As my landlady is pressing for the rent, I shall be here on Monday for the threshing machine. But you haven't heard the last of this. Good day to you. *(As he passes the dog actor)* And if you start yapping round my bedside I won't be too weak to

'The plough of
time has come to the
end of its furrow'

fetch you a vicious blow with my stick. *(He opens the door, then turns back to the assembled cast)* Untutored hams.

He slams the door behind him. Fade.

Fade up the 'On the Air' sign. It is towards end of the next episode, and the cast are in the studio, round the mike as before, with their scripts in their hands.

Dan Bowman   How is he doctor?

Doctor   I'm sorry, Mr Bowman.

Mrs Bowman   You mean, there's no chance?

Doctor   I'm sorry. We've done all we can.

George   Poor old Joshua.

Fred   I think he's trying to say something.

Dan Bowman   What is it, Joshua old son?

Tony groans weakly.

Mrs Bowman   We're here, Joshua. Your friends are here.

Tony   *(groans)* Gladys. Dan. I'm going:

Dan Bowman   No you're not, Joshua. You'll pull through. You'll soon be back at Brook Farm, your old cheerful self again.

Tony coughs, and groans some more.

Tony   *(Suffolk)* No, no, Dan, me old pal me old beauty. The plough of time has come to the end of its furrow. *(Scots)* It's harvest time and the great farmer *(Welsh)* has come to gather me in, you see. *(Robert Newton)* Aha Dan lad, I'll be in Valhalla on the noon tide . . . Ahaha.

He is nudged by the other actors, groans weakly, and continues in a variety of accents.

Tony   I'm sinking . . . it won't be long now. I'm going. When you get your beetroots in, will you think of me? I'm going.

He does a big death scene with strangulation sounds, groans, etc.

'. . . the great farmer has come to gather me in'

'Aha . . . I'll be in Valhalla on the noon tide'

Mrs Bowman Er . . . I think he's gone, Dan.

Tony *(groans loudly)* I'm going, I'm going. Goodbye Dan. Goodbye Gladys. Goodbye Fred, goodbye George. There's only one thing I'd like to ask before I go. Me last wish, me last wish. I'd like my dear old dog to be buried alongside of me.

He groans, and dies again, making another big performance of it.

Mrs Bowman I think . . . I think he's gone Dan.

Diane *(coming on mike)* Mother . . . Father, am I too late?

Dan Bowman I'm afraid you are, Diane. His poor old tired heart has finally stopped. He's gone to a better place for a long deserved rest.

Tony groans, then coughs. The other actors try to push him off mike, but he fights his way back in again.

Tony I'm still here, haven't gone yet. But I'm going. I'm going. Is that you Diane? Come to see old Joshua off on the long journey, have you? *(Coughs)* I'm going *(groans again)*.

Dan Bowman Er . . . we'd better be getting back to the farm. There's nothing more we can do here with old Joshua . . . *dead!*

Tony tries to get in again, but they stand in front of him and stop him getting to the mike. He dodges about, but they dodge with him and successfully bar his way. While the struggle goes on the following dialogue takes place.

Mrs Bowman So he's gone. Dear kind-hearted old Joshua has gone.

Dan Bowman The best friend a man ever had. Although he's gone, he'll always be with us.

Tony again attempts to get to the mike. The producer, who has come into the studio in his shirtsleeves, tries to stop him. George covers the mike with his hands as Tony approaches, and between them they manage to push him out again.

Mrs Bowman *(tearful)* Poor old Joshua.

Dan Bowman Come on love, he wouldn't want us to stand here crying over him. Let's go home.

By now the producer has his arm round Tony's neck and his hand over his mouth to ensure that he says nothing more. Tony is struggling to get free and, as the signature tune comes in, he bites the producer's hand.

Announcer You have been listening to 'The Bowmans', an everyday story of simple people. The News and Radio Newsreel follows in a few moments.

The actors all turn on Tony as soon as they are off the air. The producer is in obvious pain from Tony's bite.

Dan Bowman *(to Tony)* My word, you made a meal of that, didn't you?

Mrs Bowman Disgusting performance.

Producer This is the last time you ever work on one of my programmes.

Tony You weren't getting rid of me as easily as all that. If I was going to go, I was going in a blaze of glory. Hallo, what have we got here?

They all turn to see a new actor who has come into the studio.

Producer I'd like you all to meet Julian Court. Julian is joining the programme from tomorrow night. He plays Gregory Forrester, who buys old Joshua's farm.

Julian Court How do you do. I'm looking forward to a long and happy association with all of you.

Tony It won't be a long one, mate. As soon as you start getting popular they'll have you in the threshing machine like a shot.

Producer Mr Hancock, there's nothing more for you to do here. Would you be so good as to leave the studio?

Tony With the greatest of pleasure.

Producer Here's your money.

He hands Tony an envelope. Tony opens it.

Tony There's generosity for you. The golden handshake. Four pounds, twelve shillings and sixpence. Not even a week's wages.

Producer They are Equity rates. One day's pay. Good afternoon.

Tony goes to the studio door, then turns back.

Tony You'll regret this. You don't know what a little gem you had in me. I'm on me own now, I'll show you. It was only this hotchpotch of rural beatniks that have been holding me back. I'll get the chance to do some real acting for a change now. Good day to you.

He slams the door as he leaves. The producer starts introducing the new member of the cast.

Producer This is Windthrift Osmington.

Julian Court shakes hands with Dan Bowman.

Producer Celia Beaumont.

He shakes hands with Mrs Bowman, and the scene fades out.
Fade up a blackboard on an easel, on which is chalked 'Auditions today: Hamlet'. An actor is just finishing the soliloquy from Hamlet. He

is standing in a pool of light — the stage all round him is in darkness. Before he finishes . . .

Voice *(off)* Thank you very much. We'll let you know. Next.

Actor But I hadn't finished yet.

Voice That's quite enough for us to judge. Thank you.

Actor I have some more . . .

Voice That's quite all right, we know what you can do. Next, please.

The actor walks off, and Tony comes on. He puts down the case which he is carrying and peers out into the blackness, shielding his eyes from the footlights.

Tony Hancock. Anthony Hancock. Joshua in 'The Bowmans', an everyday story of simple people.

Voice Thank you, carry on.

Tony Yes, er . . . what would you like to hear?

Voice Well if it's all the same to you we'd like to hear the part you came to audition for.

Tony Yes, well I don't know very much about it you see. I was in the coffee bar, I may be a little rusty . . .

Voice Yes, carry on.

Tony I don't normally do auditions, you know.

Voice That's all right, carry on.

Tony leans over and opens his case. He takes out a wig, and puts it on.

Voice We don't need any props.

Tony I thought it might add to the charm of the thing, give you some idea of how I'm going to interpret the role.

'Hush, what light from yonder
window breaks?'

Voice We are familiar with the costumes of the piece, just get on with the reading.

Tony *(taking off the wig)* Certainly, I do beg your pardon. It's a long time since I did an audition.

Voice So you said. Now do hurry, come along please, we do have other people waiting.

Tony Yes, quite. *(Clears his throat)* Hush, what light from yonder window breaks? 'Tis Juliet, and the sun is in the West . . .

Voice Mr Hancock, the play is *Hamlet*.

Tony *Hamlet?* Is it? I was distinctly told *The Merchant of Venice.* I'm terribly sorry. *Hamlet* is a different cup of tea, of course. Which interpretation do you fancy?

Voice We just want the words, loud and clear. This is a British Arts Council tour of Tanganyika, I'm sure they won't worry about the interpretation.

Tony Tanganyika. I wasn't told that.

Voice Do you want the part or not?

Tony It's a few weeks in the sun, I suppose. What's the money like?

Voice Let's wait and see whether you are right for the part, shall we?

Tony Well I don't want to waste my time. I was clearing a fair whack at the BBC. I don't really want to drop below that.

Voice *(angry)* Are you going to give us a reading or not?

Tony Yes. *(Clears throat, then speaks in Joshua's voice)* To be or not to be, that be the question . . . whether 'tis nobler in the mind to suffer the slings and arrows of outrageous fortune . . .

Voice Next.

Tony Or to take arms . . . eh?

Voice I said Tanganyika, not Norfolk. We'll let you know later.

Tony Let me know later? I'm sorry, but that is not good enough.

Voice All right. We'll let you know now. No. Next.

Tony I feel I must remind you, young man, you are not dealing with any old yobidehoy, you are dealing with an actor of some merit. I just gave you the voice that captivated twenty million listeners every night for five years.

Voice We're not interested. Next please.

Tony I warn you, the Tanganyikans aren't going to like this. I am very highly thought of in Dar es Salaam. This is no way to keep the Commonwealth together. You will be playing to empty mud huts, my man. There are other managements you know. I shall offer my services to those who appreciate the talents of a true artiste.

Cut and fade up the inside of a film studio. A crew are on the film camera.

Director Action.

The camera tracks in and we see the set. There is a lovely girl in a crinoline, powdered wig, carrying a black mask on the end of a stick. Tony enters, dressed in the Rupert of Schleswig Holstein full dress uniform with monocle. He sweeps his cloak in greeting and goes up to the girl. He clicks to attention and then kisses her hand. They sink down together on to a plush divan and she caresses his cheek.

Announcer *(off)* What has he got that other men haven't?

Tony brings a tin of pilchards out from under his cloak. The camera closes in on the tin. The girl gasps in pleasure as he shows it to her. She throws her arms round him and strokes his cheek.

Announcer   Yes, Grimsby Pilchards, sought after by ladies of quality since 1811.

We see Tony looking at the camera over the girl's shoulder. He smirks and holds up the tin.

Announcer   Grimsby Pilchards, twopence off for a trial offer.

Fade out, and fade up a country scene. Tony emerges from a tent, dressed as Napoleon, with his hand inside his tunic. He rubs his stomach with his free hand.

Announcer   *(off)* Yes, Napoleon has every right to rub his tummy, he has just had a delicious meal of . . .

Tony brings his hand out of his tunic, to reveal a tin of Grimsby Pilchards. A girl, dressed as Josephine, runs up to him, throws her arms around him and strokes his cheek.

Announcer   . . . Grimsby Pilchards, the food of Emperors.

Close up of Tony looking at the camera over Josephine's shoulders. He smirks and holds up the tin.

Announcer   Grimsby Pilchards for men. Fourpence off for a trial offer.

Fade out, and fade up a dance hall. Tony, in full evening dress, walks up to a girl who is in the dance championships dress. He asks the girl to dance, but she shakes her head and dances off with a good looking boy. Tony gloomily looks after them, and then brightens up as he has an idea. He sits down and takes from his tails a tin of pilchards. He opens them with a tin opener, takes a fork and spears a bit, whereupon he is surrounded by beautiful girls all smiling at him and stroking his cheek, etc. He smiles cockily.

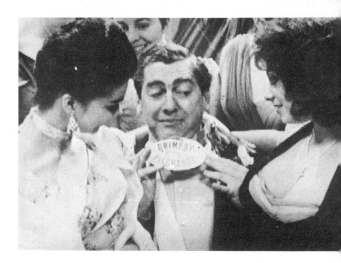

Announcer   *(off)*   Yes, you're never alone with a pilchard.

92

Tony now has a girl on each knee and another couple hanging round his neck stroking his hair and his cheek. He smirks and holds up the tin.

Announcer Grimsby Pilchards, sixpence off a trial offer.

Fade.

Fade up a shot of a graph marked 'Grimsby Pilchards Sales Campaign' with a line going straight across it. A hand comes in and draws a line downwards.

Fade up Tony's flat. He enters, and takes off his hat and coat. He slings them away, takes off his jacket and slings that away, then collapses on the bed. He is very despondant.

Tony Fools! What a liberty, giving me the push. Best advert they've ever had. They can't blame me for what's inside the tin. I told them it was the tomato sauce that's turning people off. And they should have taken the heads off. Very unnerving to open a tin and see six heads staring up at you. But no, they have to have a scapegoat, go on, blame it on the artist. When anything goes wrong, kick the actor out. Oh, show business is being run by idiots these days. No men of vision left. Oh for the days of the actor manager, my own theatre and that *(puts thumb on nose)* to all of them. They don't want talent these days. They just want a pretty face. *(Slight pause)* Not that I don't come under that category as well. I'm not a pretty boy, I agree . . . I'm more like Peter Finch. Oscar Wilde. *(Exaggerated)* 'Parsley is ghastly'. Oh I think I'll turn acting in. Go and live on a barge. It's a facile life anyway. *(Posh voice)* 'Hallo, darling, caught the show last night, loved it, you were absolutely divine.' What a load of old rubbish. I'll be a missionary I think. Help the underprivileged people of the world. I hear it pays quite well too. Or should I just do away with myself . . .

There is a knock on the door. Tony goes and opens it. A postman is standing outside, carrying an enormous sack of letters.

Postman Mr Joshua Merryweather?

Tony Who? Oh yes, yes of course.

The postman walks into the flat and heaves the sack off his shoulder and on to the floor.

Postman You caused a bit of a stink dying last night, didn't you?

Tony Last night?

Postman Yes, on the old Bowmans programme. My old woman was very cut up about it, you know.

Tony That was two weeks ago.

Postman No, last night. I heard it. Didn't you see the newspapers today? All over the front pages.

Tony Of course, the programme is recorded in advance. It didn't go out till last night.

Postman That's what I said. You've upset the whole country you have. *(Points to the sack).* Look at that. Letters of protest I shouldn't wonder. They're all up in arms about it. It's going to cost you a pretty penny to answer all those.

The postman goes out.

Tony They've all gone mad.

There is another knock on the door. Tony opens it, to find a man standing there with two large wreaths.

Man Mrs Joshua Merryweather, please.

Tony Mrs . . . ?

Man These floral tributes have been sent by sympathetic people throughout the country on the sad occasion of her husband's death.

The man walks to the table, claps his hands, and half a dozen pageboys come in, all carrying wreaths and great bunches of flowers. They put them down.

Man Ah, it's going to be a lovely funeral.

Tony *(incredulous)* This is madness.

Man There's more to come, from my establishment alone there's another six vanloads. I must say we were all very upset to hear the news. Tell Mrs Merryweather our hearts are with her in her hour of sorrow.

Tony Oh this is ridiculous. It's only a programme.

Man When is the funeral? We've all got our armbands on. Ah yes, a day of national mourning. Oh, and here's a little tribute from my good lady wife and myself. *(He hands Tony a little wreath and points to the card)* 'Joshua Merryweather. Only sleeping.' Well, I'd better get back and comfort my wife, she hasn't stopped crying since last night, and I expect you have got all the arrangements to see to. Good morning.

As he leaves, a young reporter rushes in.

Reporter Mr Hancock. I'm Tim Walters of the Evening Globe. I want to do a follow up story on tonight's main headline.

Tony What are you talking about?

Reporter Haven't you seen the papers. Look.

He hands Tony a paper, and Tony reads the headlines.

Tony *(reading)* 'Nation stunned by untimely demise of Joshua Merryweather. Thousands of listeners jam telephone lines to BBC.' *(Pleased)* Really?

'This is madness'

Reporter It's fantastic. You realise the BBC had five thousand complaints in an hour after last night's programme?

Tony *(beaming)* Get away. *(Reads again)* 'A BBC spokesman said last night . . ."we had no idea this character was so popular. The heads of department are meeting to review the situation."'

Reporter Now look, Mr Hancock. My paper would like to do a regular feature every night called The Joshua Merryweather Column, philosophical advice to the lonely and the miserable. You know, the sort of thing you've been doing on the programme, the quaint corny up against the pig sty sort of stuff . . . comments on the political situation, anything. You don't have to write it, all we want is a picture of you at the top and the name and we're willing to pay you £5000 a year.

Tony Isn't that marvellous. Four pounds twelve and six a day when you're alive, five thousand a year when you're dead.

Fade.

Fade up Broadcasting House, then dissolve to inside a conference room. A few BBC officials are sitting round the large table.

Tony sweeps in and they immediately rise to greet him.

Head official My dear sir, welcome back to Broadcasting House.

Another official holds a chair out for Tony, who sits down.

Head official Have a cigar.

Tony takes the cigar. All the others rush to light it for him, but he deliberately lights it with his own lighter.

Head official Well now, Mr Hancock, I'm sure that we won't have any difficulty with our little problem.

Tony I'm sure we won't.

Head official Yes quite. We've made tentative arrangements for the return of your character to the programme. Mr Ponsonby?

Producer Well I think you're going to like this — *(pause)* . . . Tony. Joshua has a twin brother, looks like him, all the gestures exactly identical. He suddenly turns up at Brookhampton, buys his brother's old farm and sets up in residence exactly as before.

Tony How very ingenious.

Head official You like it.

Tony Yes, I think it's a very, very, very good idea.

They all beam at each other, relieved.

Tony There's only one snag.

Head official What?

Tony I'm not doing it — *(pause)* unless . . .

Head official Yes?

Tony Unless you agree to my terms. Ten thousand a year, five year contract, I get top billing, I'll write all me own scripts, and a free radio licence.

Head official Write all your own scripts?

Tony Yes. I'm not having any more of this disappearing in the threshing machine again. Good afternoon, gentlemen, I don't think there is anything else to discuss. Your humble servant.

He takes a little bow and exits.

Fade up the inside of the studio. The rest of the Bowmans cast and Tony are standing around the mike. All but Tony look very sullen. The 'On the Air' sign goes on, the producer signals, and the signature tune begins. The announcer steps up to the mike.

Announcer We present Anthony Hancock as Old Ben Merryweather, in 'The Merryweathers', an everyday story of Old Ben Merryweather.

Actor Good morning Ben, how are you today?

Tony Oh, ahh, me old pal me old beauty.

Actor What's the weather going to be like today then, Ben?

Tony Well, I seen a crow on the wing this morning, and he went round in three circles and flew off to the North, ah it'll be raining by lunchtime.

Actor Oh look, coming across the fields. There be Dan Bowman, Mrs Bowman, their daughter Diane, and George and Fred his farmhands, the Squire and his wife, old Jim who owns the tobacconists, the Vicar, and the Manager of the Turks Head. Half the village be coming across.

Tony Dang me, they shouldn't be walking across that field.

Actor Why not?

The rest of the cast cry out in unison. This is followed by silence.

Tony *(flat)* Oh dear, what a shame. They've all fallen down that disused mine shaft.

Actor We'd better get them out.

Tony No, no, there be no point. No, no, no, no. Three hundred foot deep it is. They'll all be splattered across the bottom. Ha, ha. Fill it in and forget about them. Put some of them wreaths we had left over from Joshua on top of them.

Actor But that be half the village gone.

Tony Ah, but we'll soon stock it up again, lad. I've got a lot of relatives knocking about. I reckon I can run this village on my own. *(Sings)* I've got mangel wurzels in my garden, I've got mangel wurzels in my shed . . . I've got mangel wurzels in my bathroom, and a mangel wurzel for a head. *(Smiling broadly — Robert Newton)* Ahaaa . . . ha . . . ha . . .

Fade.

'AHAAAA . . . HA . . . HA . . . HA . . . HA . . .'

THE BLOOD DONOR

Shot of the outside of a large London hospital, then cut to a plaque showing the name of the hospital.
Dissolve to a door reading 'Blood Donor Department', and then into the room. There are a few donors awaiting attention, reading magazines etc. A nurse is sitting at a reception desk. At one end of the room is a door leading to the annexe where the blood donations are taken. Tony enters, looks round, and goes up to the reception desk.

Nurse   Good afternoon, sir.

Tony   Good afternoon, miss. I have come in answer to your advert on the wall next to the Eagle Laundry in Pelham Road.

Nurse   An advert? Pelham Road?

Tony   Yes. Your poster. You must have seen it. There's a nurse pointing at you, a Red Cross lady actually I believe, with a moustache and a beard — pencilled in, of course. You must know it, it's one of yours, it's next to 'Chamberlain Must Go', just above the cricket stumps. It says 'Your blood can save a life'.

Nurse   Oh I see, you wish to become a blood donor.

Tony   I certainly do. I've been thinking about this for a long time. No man is an island, young lady. To do one unselfish act with no thought of profit or gain is the duty of every human being. Something for the benefit of the country as a whole. What should it be, I thought. Become a blood donor or join the Young Conservatives? But as I'm not looking for a wife and I can't play table tennis, here I am. A body full of good British blood and raring to go.

Nurse   Yes, quite. Well now, would you sit down and I'll just take a few particulars. May I have your name?

Tony   *(sitting)* Yes, Hancock. Anthony Hancock. Twice candidate for the County Council elections, defeated, Hon. Sec. British Legion, Earl's Court Branch, treasurer of the darts team and the outings committee.

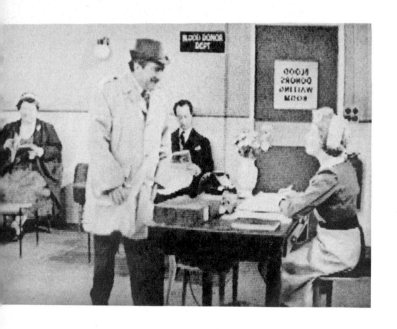

Nurse I only want the name.

Tony We're going to Margate this year — by boat. If there are any young nurses like yourself who would care to join us, we would be more than happy to accommodate you. No nonsense, you know what I mean.

Nurse Thank you, I'll bear it in mind. Now, date of birth?

Tony Er, yes. Shall we say the twelfth of May, nineteen er . . . I always remember the twelfth of May. It was Coronation Day, you know, nineteen thirty-six.

Nurse You're only twenty-five?

Tony No, no, no, no, the Coronation was in nineteen thirty-six. I was born a little before that in, er, nineteen er . . . *(Makes a quick mental calculation)* Is all this really necessary?

Nurse Yes, I'm afraid so. The twelfth of May . . .

Tony Yes. I always remember that, the Coronation, we all got a day off at our school . . . did you? And we got a cup and saucer in a box and a bar of soap. Very good, I've still got that today, and a spoon for the Silver Jubilee and a biscuit tin with their pictures on . . .

Nurse How old are you?

Tony *(disgruntled)* Thirty-five.

Nurse Thank you. Nationality?

Tony Ah, you've got nothing to worry about there. It's blood you're thinking about, isn't it? British. British. Undiluted for twelve generations. One hundred per cent Anglo-Saxon, with perhaps just a dash of Viking, but nothing else has crept in. No, anybody who gets any of this will have nothing to complain about. There's aristocracy in there, you know. You want to watch who you're giving it to . . . It's like motor oil, it doesn't mix, if you get my meaning.

Nurse Mr Hancock, when a blood transfusion is being given, the family background is of no consequence.

Tony Oh come now, surely you don't expect me to believe that. I mean after all east is east, really . . .

Nurse *(slightly needled)* And blood is blood, Mr Hancock, all over the world. It is classified by groups and not by accidents of birth.

Tony I did not come here for a lecture on Communism, young lady.

Nurse I happen to be a Conservative.

Tony Then kindly behave like one, madam.

Nurse Have you had any of these diseases?

She hands him a printed list, which Tony reads. He tries to remember a couple of the names on it. Looks puzzled by one, then uncomfortable at another, then indignant at another.

Tony How dare you! *(Starts to hand the list back)* No I have not. (Points) Especially that one. I told you before you have nothing to fear from me. I am perfectly healthy. Fit? Fit? If we'd had our own rocket, I'd've been the first one up there. I had my name down for Blue Streak, but no, we missed our chance again. It's not right having these foreigners hurtling round up there, you mark my words . . .

Nurse Blood, Mr Hancock, blood.

Tony Eh? Yes. Ah, yes. I beg your pardon, I do get carried away over things like that, it's a sore point with me. *(Eager)* Are we ready now then?

'One hundred per cent Anglo-Saxon with perhaps just a dash of Viking'

Nurse There is just one more thing. Have you given any blood before?

Tony Given, no. Spilt, yes. Yes, there's a good few drops lying about on the battlefields of Europe. Are you familiar with the Ardennes? *(Nurse looks up, startled)* I well remember Von Runstedt's last push — Tiger Harrison and myself, being in a forward position, were cut off behind the enemy lines. 'Captain Harrison,' I said. 'Yes sir,' he said. *(Nurse raises an eyebrow)* 'Jerry's overlooked us,' I said. 'Where shall we head for?' 'Berlin,' he said. 'Right,' I said. 'Last one in the Reichstag is a sissy.' So we set off . . . got there three days before the Russians . . .

Nurse You've never been a blood donor before.

Tony Yes. No. So — there we were, surrounded by Storm Troopers. 'Kamerad, Kamerad,' they said . . .

The nurse has not taken any notice of this, and now hands him a card.

Nurse If you will just sit over there with the others, Doctor will call you when he's ready.

Tony Oh. Thank you. Over here?

Nurse Yes.

She gets up, puts some papers under her arm, and leaves the room. Tony makes his way over to the chairs where two other donors, a man and a woman, are waiting. He sits down on the chair between them, and looks round.

Tony Well — it's a grand job we're all doing. *(Pause)* Yes, I think we can all be very proud of ourselves. *(Pause)* Some people, all they do is take, take, take out of life, and never put anything back. Well that's not my way of living, and never has been. Never has been. You're only entitled to take out of life what you are prepared to put into it. *(To man)* Do we get a badge for doing this?

Man No, I don't think so.

Tony Pity. We should have something for people to pick us out by.

Man Not really important, is it? As long as we give the blood and help someone, that's the main thing.

Tony Oh well, quite, quite. I mean as long as they get their corpuscles, quite, quite. That's reward in itself, I agree, no names, no pack drill, quite, quite. I just think we ought to get a badge as well. I mean nothing grand, a little enamelled thing, a little motto that's all, nothing pretentious, something like 'He gaveth for others so that others may live'.

The man is obviously finding all this very distasteful.

Tony You know, I mean we are do-gooders, we should get something for it.

Man What do you want, money?

Tony Don't be vulgar. I am a great believer in charity. Help others, that's my motto. I contribute to every flag day that's going. The lapels of my suits are always the first thing to go. Covered in holes they are. Yes I always give what I can. *(Brings out his diary)* Have a look at this, it's all in me diary. Congo Relief, two and six, Self-denial Week, one and eight, Lifeboat Day, a tanner, Arab Refugees, one and two. Yes it's all down here . . . yes . . . yes . . . I do what I can. My conscience is clear. And when I'm finally called, by the Great Architect, and he says 'What did you do?' I shall just bring me book out, and say, 'Here you are, mate, add that lot up.' Yes, I mean I've got nothing to fear, no, I could go tomorrow. Ah yes, let's see.

He takes a pencil from the spine of the diary and makes an entry.

Tony October, 1961. Gave blood for the needy. How much do you reckon that's worth? Three quid? Just to keep the books straight, you know. Just for my own benefit, I'm not trying to put a price on it.

The man reacts in disgust. Tony puts the diary back and relaxes, very pleased with himself.

Tony Do you come here often?

Man This is my twelfth time.

Tony Well there's no need to boast about it, old man. How much did you give to the Arab Refugees?

Man Oh really.

Tony No come on, how much? You're shout-

ing about how much blood you've given, how much did you give to the Arab Refugees?

Man If you must know, I gave five pounds.

Pause.

Tony Oh. Well there you are. I mean some people are better placed than others.

Man Well let's forget about it, shall we?

Tony Well yes, all right.

Man I find the whole thing distasteful.

Tony All right, all right.

A different nurse has come to the door of the annexe.

2nd Nurse Mr Johnson. Doctor's ready for you now. You know the way, don't you.

Man Yes, thank you.

The man gets up and goes into the annexe. Tony turns to the large woman sitting on his other side, who is reading a magazine.

Tony   A bit of a bighead, isn't he?

Woman Who?

'And when I'm finally called, by the Great Architect,
and he says "What did you do?" I shall just bring me book out,
and say, Here you are mate, add that lot up'

'AHAHA'

Tony Him! If you can't give to charity without shouting about it from the rooftops, well . . . Is this your first time?

Woman I come here every six months. For the last twelve years.

Tony Oh well, you've got a bit to spare, haven't you? I mean a person of your size . . . too much blood is as bad as too little I always say.

Woman Are you trying to be insulting?

Tony No, no nothing personal. Just an observation. I think it is very laudable to give so much. Of course some people make it up quicker than others. I mean, I expect you're a big eater. It wouldn't take you long to recoup the er . . . I mean a woman of your build . . . that is to say . . . I mean . . . they've certainly brightened these hospitals up, haven't they. Of course it's the Health Service that's done that. They spend more money on paint. Out of every thirteen and six paid in, sixpence halfpenny goes up on the wall. Well it's worth it, I mean . . .

2nd Nurse Mrs Forsythe, Doctor's ready for you now. Would you come this way?

The woman gets up and follows the nurse.

Tony *(calls after her)* Best of luck. Just think, Cliff Richard might get yours. *(To himself)* That'd slow him down a bit.

Tony settles back in his chair and hums to himself. He starts looking around for something to do. Spends some time hitting his leg just below the kneecap, trying to get a reflex reaction from his leg. He gives that up and gets up from his chair, looking around the room again. There are some posters on the walls — 'Have you been immunized?' 'Keep death off the road', etc. He walks over to a poster advertising milk.

Tony Drink-a pint-a milk-a day. *(Faster)* Drink-a-pint-a-milk-a-day. *(Faster still)* Drinkapintamilkaday!

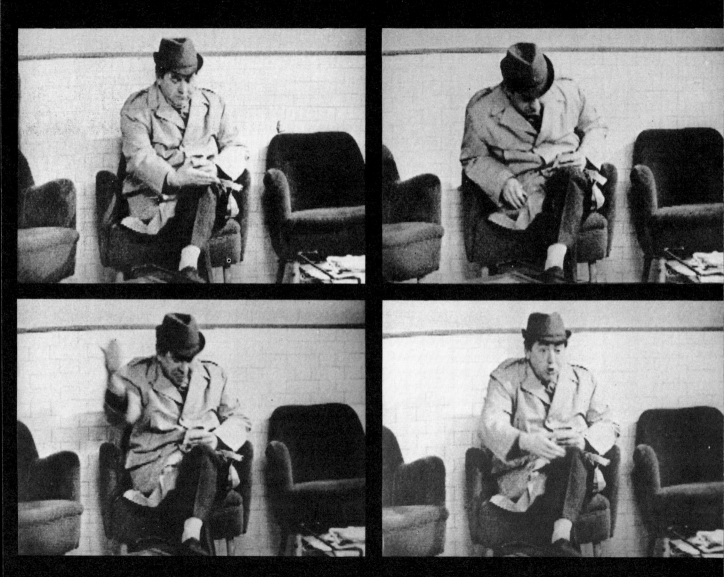

The reception desk nurse comes back and sits down at her desk, a few yards away from Tony. He hasn't noticed her, and now turns his attention to another poster.

Tony *(recites)* Coughs and sneezes spread diseases. *(Sings to the tune of 'Deutschland Uber Alles' and starts goose-stepping)* Coughs and sneezes spread diseases, trap the germs in your handkerchief, coughs and sneezes spread . . .

Nurse Are you all right?

Tony Oh, I'm sorry. Hello Nurse, didn't see you come back. I, er, felt rather lonely sitting here by myself. It's funny what you do when you're on your own, isn't it? Just looking at the posters. *(Laughs in embarrassment)* Is, er . . . is this a normal sort of day for you then? Do you get many people in normally or is this, er . . . er . . . normal?

Nurse *(without looking up from her work)* It's about average.

Tony Yes, quite. Quite. I mean it's a vocation, nursing, I've always said that. One of the highest callings a woman can aspire to.

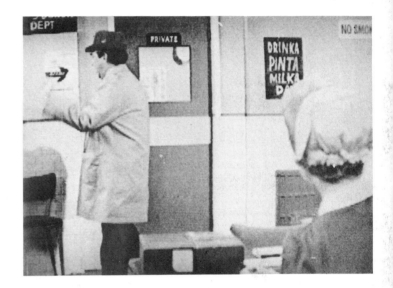

Bored reaction from the nurse.

Tony Well I mean it's not the money, for you, is it? It's strange isn't it, the different values we place on society. I mean you take modelling for instance. Now just take modelling. You get some skinny bird, up in the West End, all bones and salt cellars, dragging a piece of fur along a platform — fifty quid a week. And there's you lot, dedicated, three years' training, humping great trolly loads of mince about all day long. It's not right. Now is it right? There's Adam Faith earning ten times as much as the Prime Minister. Is that right? *(Emphatically)* Is that right? Mind you, I suppose it depends on whether you like Adam Faith and what your politics are.

The nurse continues to work throughout this, not taking the slightest bit of notice.

**'There's Adam Faith
earning ten times as much
as the Prime Minister.
Is that right?'**

Tony I understand you get a cup of tea and a biscuit afterwards.

Nurse Yes.

Pause.

Tony But no badge.

Nurse No.

Tony They're taking their time in there, aren't they? Everything's all right, I suppose.

Nurse Yes.

Tony Just wondered. I just thought some of the poor devils might pass out at the sight of the needle. I've seen it before. Men built like oak trees, keeling over like saplings in a hurricane. It's quite nasty.

Nurse Needles don't bother you then?

Tony Me? No. I've had too many of them, my dear. I've had the lot. I've got arms like pin cushions. Yes, I reckon I've had a syringeful of everything that's going in my time.

Needles the size of drainpipes, some of them. You name it, I've had it.

The other Nurse comes out.

2nd Nurse Well, Mr Hancock, Doctor is ready for you now.

Tony Who, me? Um . . . now? Yes, well. I mean is there . . . there's nobody else before me? I'm in no hurry. *(Looks round)* Does anybody want to go first?

2nd Nurse There isn't anybody else, you're the last one.

Tony Oh. Yes. Well . . . this is it then. *(To the first nurse)* Over the top!

They start towards the annexe where the doctor is waiting.

Tony *(confidential)* What's he like on the needle, this bloke. Steady hand?

2nd Nurse There's nothing to worry about.

Tony Is he in a good mood?

2nd Nurse You'll be quite all right. Doctor MacTaggart is an excellent doctor.

> ## 'Oh. Yes. Well . . . this is it then. Over the top!'

Tony MacTaggart! He's a Scotsman! Ah well, that's all right. Marvellous doctors the Scots, like their engineers, you know . . . It's the porridge that does it. Lead on, MacDuff!

She leads him into the annexe where the doctor is sitting at a table. By him are all the paraphernalia required for blood donations.

Nurse Mr Hancock —

Tony Ah, guid morning, it's a braw bricht moonlicht nicht the morning, mista, it's a bonny wee lassie ye got there helping you, hoots mon . . . and och aye te ye the noo.

Doctor *(educated English accent)* Would you mind sitting down there, Mr Hancock.

Tony Oh, I beg your pardon for lapsing into the vernacular, but the young lady did say you were a Scottish gentleman.

Doctor Yes, well we're not all Rob Roys. May I have your card please?

Tony By all means. *(He sits down and hands his card to the doctor)* I'm ready when you are, Squire.

The doctor looks at the card.

Doctor Good. Hold your hand out, please.

Tony holds his hand out. The doctor cleans Tony's thumb and then picks up the needle.

Doctor Now this won't hurt. You'll just feel a slight prick on the end of your thumb.

Tony winces in readiness, screwing his eyes shut.
Cut to the doctor as he jabs the needle in. Tony winces again, then has a look at the end of his thumb. He beams proudly.

Tony Dear oh dear. Well that's that, I'll have my cup of tea and my biscuit now. Nothing to it, is there, really. I can't understand why everybody doesn't do it. *(Gets up)* Well, I'll bid you good day, thank you very much,

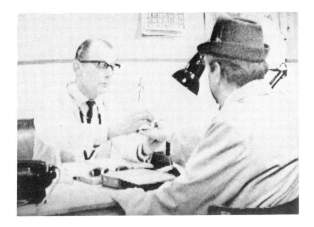

whenever you want any more, don't hesitate to get in touch with me.

Doctor Where are you going?

Tony To have my tea and biscuits.

Doctor I thought you came here to give some of your blood.

Tony You've just had it.

Doctor That is just a smear.

Tony It may be just a smear to you, mate, but it's life and death to some poor wretch.

Doctor No, no, no. I've just taken a small sample to test.

Tony A sample? How much do you want then?

Doctor Well a pint, of course.

Tony A pint? Have you gone raving mad? Oh well of course . . . I mean you must be joking.

Doctor A pint is a perfectly normal quantity to take.

Tony You don't seriously expect me to believe that. I mean, I came in here in all good faith to help my country. I don't mind giving a reasonable amount, but a pint . . . why that's very nearly an armful. I'm sorry. I'm not walking around with an empty arm for any anybody. I mean, a joke's a joke . . .

Doctor Mr Hancock, obviously you don't know very much about the workings of the human body. You won't have an empty arm, or an empty anything. The blood is circulating all the time. A normal healthy individual can give a pint of blood without any ill effects whatsoever. You do have eight pints, you know.

Tony Now look, chum, everybody to his own trade, I'll grant you, but if I've got eight pints, obviously I need eight pints, and not seven, as I will have by the time you've finished with me. No, I'm sorry, I've been misinformed, I've made a mistake. I'll do something else, I'll be a Traffic Warden . . .

Doctor Well of course I can't force you to donate your blood, but it's a great shame. You're AB Negative.

Tony Is that bad?

Doctor Oh no, no. You're rhesus positive.

Tony Rhesus? They're monkeys, aren't they? How dare you! What are you implying? I didn't come here to be insulted by a legalised vampire.

Doctor Mr Hancock, that is your blood group. AB Negative. It is one of the rarest groups there is.

Tony *(pleased)* Really.

Doctor Yes it is. Very rare indeed.

Tony Oh. Well of course I'm not surprised. I've always felt instinctively that I was somehow different from the rest of the herd. Something apart. I never fitted into society. I've never belonged if you know what I mean, the contact was never there. I was always a bit of an outsider. Well that explains it, AB Negative. One of nature's aristocrats.

Doctor I really think you ought to reconsider your decision.

Tony Yes, well of course this does throw a different complexion on the matter. Well I mean, if I am one of the few sources, one doesn't like to hog it all, so to speak. I'm not un-Christian. Very rare, eh?

Doctor Yes, and I assure you there will be no ill effects. You'll make up the deficiency in no time at all.

Tony Oh well, in that case, I'll do it. I mean, we AB Negatives must stick together. A minority group like us, we could be persecuted.

Doctor Thank you very much, Mr Hancock, I'm most grateful. Now, if you would just take off your coat and lie down over there, it won't take very long. Afterwards you rest for half an hour and then you're free to go.

Tony lies down on the bed. The nurse wheels the blood taking apparatus over. Tony watches apprehensively.

Doctor Just roll up your sleeve.

Tony does so. The Doctor starts preparing the apparatus, and then dabs Tony's arm with cotton wool.

Tony As a matter of interest, what group are you?

Doctor Group A.

Tony *(reacts disparagingly)* Huh.

Doctor *(off)* Now this won't hurt . . . relax . . .

In close up, Tony tenses himself, relaxes at the command, then winces as the needle goes in, screwing his face up. He has a look down at his arm and then turns his head away, feeling weak. He faints. Fade.

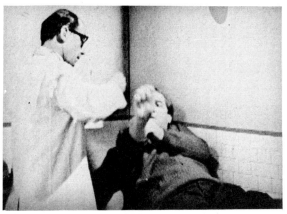

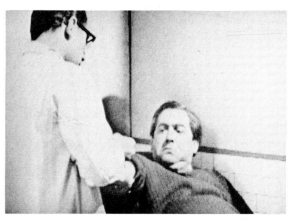

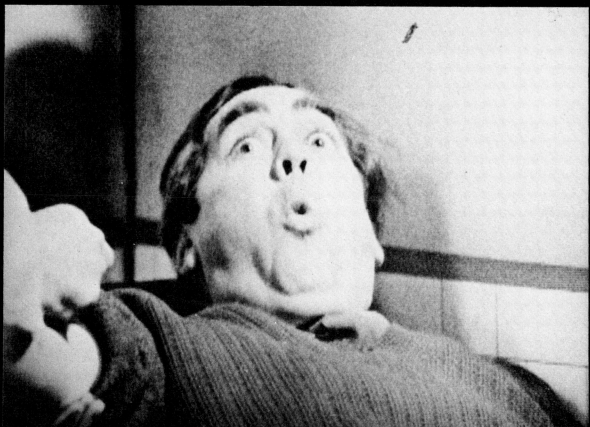
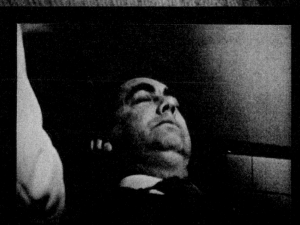

*Fade up a long room with a row of beds along
one wall. All of them are occupied by blood
donors, fully dressed and on top of the covers.
Some people are drinking tea. We see the two
Tony was speaking to earlier, and then we see
Tony. He is lying flat out on his bed. A little
man is lying on the bed next to him.*

Tony *(coming round)* Oh, where am I . . .

Nurse You're all right, you fainted that's all.

Tony *(indignant)* I did not. I was asleep —
I've been up all night.

Nurse Here's a nice cup of tea for you. A cup
of tea Mr Thomas?

Man Yes, thank you, Nurse. *(To Tony)* Are
you all right?

Tony Hmm? Oh yes, yes, fine. Nothing to it.
What group are you?

Man Group B. What group are you?

Tony *(proudly)* AB Negative.

Man Oh. That's very rare.

Tony *(cocky)* I know, I know. It's a funny
thing, this blood business.

Man Yes, I suppose it is.

Tony It all looks the same and yet . . . it's all
different. Yes, it's very funny stuff, blood.

Man Yes. I don't know where we'd be
without it.

Tony That's true. That's very true. Where
would we be without it. Yes, it's very important, blood. It circulates right round the body
you know.

Man Yes, so I believe.

Tony Yes, it starts at the heart, it gets pump-
ed right round, goes through the lungs, back
into the heart, and round it goes again.

Man What for?

Tony What for. Well it speaks for itself,
doesn't it? I mean, the heart's got to have
something to pump round. I mean there's no
point in it banging away all day long for no
reason at all.

Man Well why have a heart then?

Tony Well if you didn't the blood wouldn't
go round, would it? I mean, it'd all stay in one
place. When you stood up, it'd all sink to the
bottom of your legs. Well, it'd be very uncomfortable wouldn't it? It'd feel as if you were
walking around with a bootful of water. See,
your heart saves you from having to stand on
your head, and jumping about to keep it
moving. It does it all for you.

Man I still don't see what good blood is
though.

Tony Well look. Your body's full of veins,
isn't it?

Man Yeah.

Tony Well, you've got to fill them up with
something, haven't you?

Man Oh, I see. Are you a doctor then?

Tony Well no, not really. I never really
bothered.

Man Oh.

Tony Anything else troubling you? Any
aches and pains?

Man No, no. I'm all right.

Tony Ah well, that's the main thing isn't it.
Yes — as long as you've got your health.

Man Nothing else matters, really, does it?

Tony No it does not. And the funny thing is,
you know, you never appreciate it till you
haven't got it anymore.

'That's true.
That's very true.
Where would
we be
without it'

Man Yes, some people take their health for granted, don't they?

Tony Do you know, that could have been me talking, you took the words right out of my mouth. Yes, if you haven't got your health you haven't got anything.

Man Mind you, they do some marvellous things these days.

Tony Oh yes, it's advanced a lot, medical science. I was glad to see the back of those leeches. Yes, that was the turning point. I mean look at the things they can do these days. New blood, plastic bones, false teeth, glasses, wigs . . . do you know there's some people walking about with hardly anything they started out with.

Man Yes, what would we do without doctors, eh?

Tony Yes. *(Making a point)* Or, conversely, what would they do without us?

Man That's true. That's very shrewd.

Tony The main thing is . . . look after yourself.

Man You look after your body and your body will look after you.

Tony That's very wise. Of course the Greeks — they knew all about this years ago.

Man Did they really?

Tony Oh yes, very advanced people the Greeks were. They had hot and cold water and drains, always washing themselves they were. Of course it all got lost in the wars.

Man When Mussolini moved in.

Tony No, no, before him surely? Wasn't it? They taught it to the Romans, and the Romans came over here . . .

Man Well you can always learn from other people, can't you?

Tony Yes, of course you can. That's why I'm in favour of the Common Market. You can't ignore the rest of the world.

Man That's true. That's very true.

Tony You can't go through life with your head buried in the sand.

Man No man is an island.

Tony You're right there. I agree. Necessity is the mother of invention.

Man It certainly is. Life would be intolerable if we knew everything.

Tony I should say it would. My goodness yes. Let the shipwrecks of others be your sea marks.

Man For things unknown there is no desire.

Tony Well exactly. And then again a bird in the hand is worth two in the bush.

Man It is indeed.

Tony reaches in his pocket and offers the man a packet of wine gums.

Tony Do you like the wine gums?

Man Thank you very much.

Tony Don't take the black one.

Man No, all right. Of course they do a tube with all black ones now you know.

Tony I know, but you can't always get them.

Man Well, that's the way it goes.

Tony Still — as long as we've got our health.

Man Yes, that's the main thing.

Tony Yes, that's the main thing. Ah yes. Yes indeed.

Man Well I think I'm ready now.

Let the
shipwrecks
of others
be your
seamarks'

And then again
a bird in
the hand
is worth two
in the bush'

'Do you like
wine gums?'

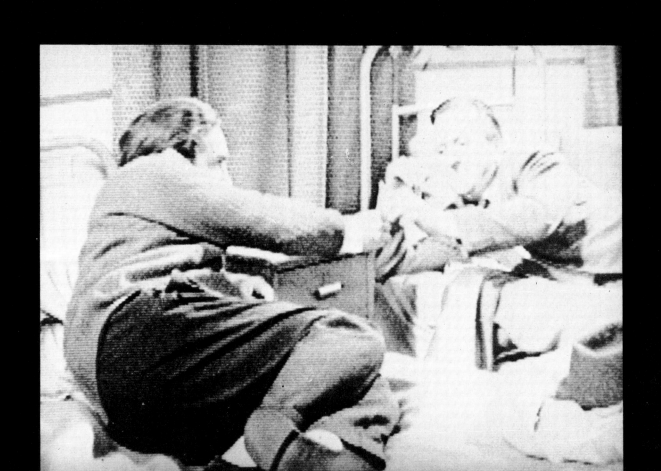

Tony Oh, you're off then.

Man Yes, out into the big world.

Tony Do you live far?

Man Just up the road.

Tony You'll get a bus then, will you?

Man No I think I'll walk.

Tony You haven't got far to go then?

Man No just up the road.

Tony Well it's not worth it then, is it.

Man Not really.

Tony Oh . . . well I'll say cheerio then.

Man Yes, cheerio. Look after yourself.

Tony Yes, and you.

Man I will.

Tony Don't do anything I wouldn't do, will you. *(Laughs)*

Man I won't. Well cheerio then.

The man leaves.

Tony Yes, nice man that, a very nice man. Very intelligent. Good conversationalist. A cut above the type you meet down the pub. A very nice man. *(Feels in his pocket)* He's walked off with my wine gums. I only broke them open for him. Oh, what's the use, if you can't trust blood donors who can you trust. Oi! Nurse! What about some tea down here, you've had me blood, it's not asking for much is it, really. And two spoonfuls of brown sugar . . . dear oh dear . . .

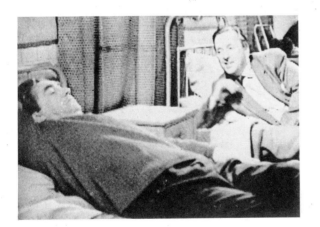

'Don't do anything I wouldn't do'

'Has it gone yet? Have you used it? Me blood!'

Fade out and fade up Tony's flat. He is dialling on the phone.

Tony Hallo, South London General? Doctor MacTaggart, please. Blood Donor Department. *(Hums to himself)* Hallo doctor, Hancock here. Yes it is me again. Has it gone yet? Have you used it? Me blood! Well you've had it twenty-four hours now, you said it was rare, surely someone must be after it. Well of course it's got something to do with me. It's my blood. Well all right, was. But you can't expect my interest in it to cease just because you've got it. Well it's a waste of time giving it if it's just going to lay about in a bottle for years. I wish to make sure it goes to the right sort of person. I wouldn't like to think of any old yobide-hoy having my blood coursing through his veins. Well really, I never thought I'd hear that sort of language from a doctor. Have you been at the meths again? Control yourself sir, there might be nurses listening. Civility costs nothing, my man. I shall phone when I like. I shall phone tomorrow, and the day after, and the day after that, and every day until my blood is used. Good day to you. *(Slams down the receiver)* Cor, what a way to speak to a blood donor.

He goes into the kitchen.

Tony If I have any more of his old buck I shall go straight to the Hospital Management Committee and have his licence taken away. I think it's reasonable to want to know where your life's blood has gone to. Especially a rare group like mine. Ah, I think I'll cut myself a sandwich.

He finds a knife and begins to cut through a loaf of bread.

Tony Got to get my strength back. A pint of blood takes some making up. Oh this bread knife's useless. Couldn't get through half a pound of butter with this. Where's that sharpener?

He looks round for the sharpener, finds it, and starts to sharpen the knife. Fade.

We see an ambulance tearing through the streets with its siren going, then the inside of a casualty ward in the hospital.

Tony is lying on a stretcher wrapped in blankets with his hand swathed in bandages and a tourniquet on his arm. A doctor comes in and takes Tony's report card from a nurse.

Doctor   Knife wound, eh. Teddy boy, is he?

Nurse   No, I don't think so. His landlady found him. Cut himself with a bread knife and fainted.

Doctor   Lost a lot of blood I see.

Nurse   Yes.

Doctor   We'll have to give him a transfusion.

Nurse   He had his blood donor's card on him. He's group AB Negative.

Doctor   Really. That's very rare. Have we got any?

Nurse   Yes, we've got just one pint in stock.

Doctor   Good. Get it, will you, nurse?

The Doctor goes over to Tony.

Doctor   Well, you're going to be all right old man. We're going to give you a transfusion.

Tony   *(weakly)* I'm a very rare blood group you know.

Doctor   Yes, yes, we know. We've got just one pint of your group in stock — you're to have that.

Doctor MacTaggart comes in.

MacTaggart   Who wants the pint of AB Negative?

Doctor   Over here.

MacTaggart *(spots Tony)* Oh no, it's not for him.

Doctor Why?

MacTaggart He only gave it yesterday. *(To Tony)* Waste of time, wasn't it?

Tony Well I would have been in a right state if I hadn't, there's nothing else here for me. At least I know it's going to the right sort of person. These blood banks. They're like ordinary banks really. Put it in when you're flush, draw it out when you need it. Come on, bang it in, I'm getting dizzy. I'll let you have it back later on. *(To nurse)* What's on the menu tonight? You got any mince? I like mince, particularly hospital mince . . .

Fade.

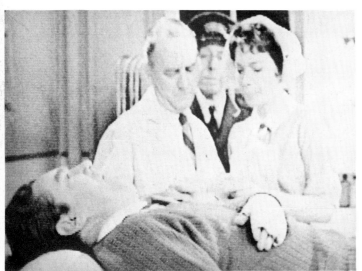 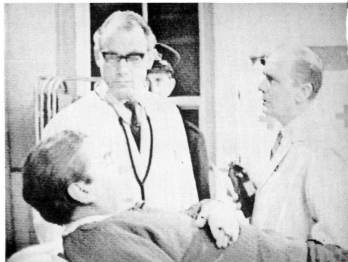

'Come on,
bang it in,
I'm getting dizzy'

RAY GALTON AND ALAN SIMPSON

in conversation with Colin Webb

How did you start writing together?

Simpson Well in the sanatorium where we met there was a closed-circuit radio network which had been built by one of the blokes there, Tony Wallis. His two-bed cubicle was like an engineering workshop — power drills, lathes, one complete wall of spare parts and tools, the lot. All against the rules. While the staff had their backs turned he re-wired the whole sanatorium, clambering over the rooftops clad only in his dressing gown and pyjamas. And when he'd finished, every patient had the choice of three programmes: the equivalent of the Home Service, the Light Programme and this third circuit which was the sanatorium network. There was a little radio room full of records which were provided by the Friends of the Sanatorium and really all they did was play record request programmes for the patients, as well as information, competition winners, messages from relatives, etc. And then a radio committee was formed and Ray and I were on it. We all decided to try and be more ambitious in the type of programmes we were putting out to the network. For example, we started a weekly cinema show — we'd take the current film that was showing and do 'A Seat in the Circle', where we'd plug into the soundtrack and one of us would say 'and Humphrey Bogart has now opened the door and walked across the room' and, you know, do a commentary between the dialogue. We also did a sort of radio 'Grandstand', doing commentaries on the tennis matches between the nurses and the doctors. We used to have bands like Harry Gold and his Pieces of Eight visit us; Steve Race would come down and give musical lectures in the main hall and we used to plug them into the network so they were broadcast to the bed-ridden patients. Then Ray and I undertook to write some comedy scripts, and we wrote them and broadcast them ourselves from this little radio room.

Were you influenced by any radio comedy programmes that were going out at the time?

Galton Yes, very influenced. We used to listen to everything. Every programme that

126

was broadcast by the BBC, then after lights out we would switch on to another illicit network that we had rigged up. The same bloke who put up the sanatorium system had a big ex-RAF 1155 radio screwed to his bedside wall and we used to tune in to AFM Munich, Stuttgart from, say, about four o'clock in the afternoon — in the winter-time anyway, because you could get better reception after dark — and listen to all the American comedy programmes. That network only went out to a privileged few who were close to the bedside of this maniac. We would listen till one or two o'clock in the morning. Our problem was to keep him awake so that he would turn the set off.

Simpson We listened to The Jack Benny Show, The Phil Harris Show, The Bob Hope Show — they all had their own half-hour situation comedies.

Galton Duffy's Tavern, George Gobel, The Great Gildersleeve, really obscure stuff.

Simpson Ozzie and Harriet, Amos 'n' Andy, The Don Ameche Show, Henry Morgan.

When did you start writing professionally?

Simpson Well having been very interested in all these comedy shows and then having done our little stint of writing for the sanatorium, Ray and I wrote a letter to Frank Muir and Denis Norden from the sanatorium asking how you became a scriptwriter. They were already established with 'Take It From Here' which had started in 1948 and was the biggest thing in British radio at that time. We listened to that every week, and it was always my favourite programme. Anyway, they wrote back — as we write back now to those kinds of letters — saying 'Thank you very much for your kind comments, the best thing to do is to send any material you've got in to the Script Editor of the BBC who is Gale Pedrick and is always on the lookout for new writers.' So that was that. Then we came out of the sanatorium and I became involved in a church hall concert party which I'd done bits and pieces for before I'd gone into the sanatorium.

They asked if we could do some sketches for them, so Ray and I got together again to write; this was about a year after we'd come out. We'd seen each other all the time in that year, but we hadn't thought any more about writing. I'd gone back to work on a part-time basis and Ray wasn't working, so he used to come over to my house in the evenings and we wrote these sketches. Then having got back together again to write we decided to send a sketch in to Gale Pedrick at the BBC. We wrote about a 15-page sketch which was based on the last part of 'Take It From Here' when they used to do a satire or a take-off on a current film — 'The African Queen' or whatever it was. We wrote one based on Henry Morgan the Pirate for three people — Joy Nichols, Dick Bentley and Jimmy Edwards.

Do you remember what each of you contributed to the script at that stage? Was the relationship clear right from the start?

Simpson The modus operandi was exactly the same as it is now, as I remember. I used to do the actual writing down of the things, as I do the typing now. Everything was thrown backwards and forwards, and when a line was agreed it went down. We didn't have a typewriter.

And what developed?

Simpson Well, we sent the sketch in and Gale Pedrick wrote back and said that they found it very amusing and would we go up and have a chat with him. I came home and read this letter and I immediately hopped on a bus and rushed over to Ray's waving the letter and all our friends read the letter and we all got drunk that night.

Galton The mere fact of getting a letter from the BBC — it was the most exciting thing that had ever happened to us.

Simpson We made the appointment and went up to see Gale Pedrick. He was very kind and helpful, and said he'd see if he could put us in the way of some producers who might want odd bits and pieces of material. One of the pro-

ducers he sent the sketch to was a man called Roy Speer, who was just about to start producing a new radio series called 'Happy Go Lucky' with Derek Roy. Apparently the sketch was on his desk one day when Derek went in to discuss things and he picked it up and read it and said 'What's this?', you know. The outcome was that Derek said he was doing this show and he needed some material for his own single spot and would we like to write jokes. You know, pick a subject and write as many jokes as we could think of. So we did. We went home and thought of jokes — my wife jokes, fat jokes, thin jokes, anything. Then we'd get paid for the ones he chose — we used to get five shillings a joke.

Was that the same year you first met Hancock?

Simpson He was in that particular show.

What was he doing in the show?

Galton He was . . . actually, the show was ill-conceived, an hour's duration, and though we were asked to contribute to the show, our hopes were dashed almost immediately because Derek found two writers by himself. First there were a couple of blokes who worked for the Scottish Daily Express and then when they left, two Australians were brought in, and one of the Australians was the writer who provided the sketch that Hancock appeared in. It was a Scoutmaster sketch. And it had been a big success in Australia years before, so he was doing it over here with Hancock and Graham Stark, Peter Butterworth, Bill Kerr, Dick Emery — all in this particular sketch, in one part of the show. Towards the end of the series, which was thirteen in number, the show was for various reasons getting worse and worse, and I remember that the Head of Light Entertainment, radio, at the BBC, came down and gave a stirring show business speech to the assembled cast. This was our first glimpse into proper show business. It was a corny speech, but people were crying and cheering by the end of it. And he'd also

brought in a new producer, who happened to be Dennis Main Wilson, who immediately looked around for new writers. And we were more or less standing in the background and he said to us 'Do you think you could write the three remaining shows?' The whole thing, except for the Scoutmaster sketch. We swallowed and said 'Yes'. We didn't really think that we could but the fee was 40 guineas a show, which meant about 120 quid, so we couldn't turn that down. We went home and worried like mad, but started working on it.

Simpson I gave in my notice at the office.

Galton And I think we bought a typewriter with the first fee.

Were you particularly aware of Hancock's presence as such or was he just one of the team of comics?

Galton Well during that whole thirteen weeks he spoke to us once, and that was during the last programme. We passed in the gangway of the Playhouse Theatre and he asked, 'Did you write that sketch?' And we said 'Yes', and he said 'Very funny' and walked on. That was our sole communication with him during that time.

Simpson Hancock was already established in 'Educating Archie' as the schoolmaster, and I think 'Happy Go Lucky' was in between Archies.

When did your writing and Hancock actually come together?

Simpson Well not for a while after that. Because we'd written those three last hour-long programmes, our names were put down on the BBC's list of writers who could handle a series. But for the next six months all we did was write single sketches for various comics, Derek Roy mainly.

Galton We'd write five- or ten-minute routines for things like 'Workers' Playtime'. Music Hall, that sort of thing. And then we had a call out of the blue from Jacques Brown, who was the producer of a very successful show called 'Calling All Forces'. It'd been running for about 80 weeks I think, non-stop. At that time Hancock was sharing the show with Charlie Chester. And Jacques Brown said that the writers were getting rather tired and they wanted a holiday and did we think we could write the last six shows. We hadn't been in the Forces and we thought, 'God, is it possible for us to write a comedy round the Forces?' But again we said 'Yes, we could'. So that was the first time we wrote for Hancock.

Simpson   This was a tremendous break.

Galton   This was *the* break.

Simpson   They were the two top shows on radio — 'Take It From Here' and 'Calling All Forces'. And 'Calling All Forces' was an enormous show, you know, a type of Sunday Night at the London Palladium show. There were 30 million listeners.

Was this still Variety material?

Simpson   Some of it was. It was an hour's show, with Chester and Tony Hancock fronting it . . . Charlie Chester wrote his own patter so we didn't have to worry about that. We had to write a sketch between Charlie Chester and Hancock, then a sketch with the guest instrumentalist, a sketch with the guest singer, then an introductory sketch for Hancock, Chester and their guest comic, and then the main final sketch which would be, as was the tradition in those days, a take-off of a film or a play — Murder on the Orient Express with Tony Hancock as the hero, and that would last about ten minutes.

Did Hancock have any particular image at this time?

Simpson   Yes, he'd already established an image, still based really on the schoolmaster, Archie Andrews' tutor.

Galton   And in Cockney as well —'ello,'ello, 'ello . . .

Simpson   He used to drop his aitches. 'ancock.

So when you started writing for him on this you more or less conformed to the established image.

Simpson   Oh completely. When 'Calling All Forces' finished, the BBC kept the same format going but called it 'Forces' All Star Bill'.

Galton   Charlie Chester left, and Hancock was the star.

Simpson   We wrote, I think, three out of the eight for the first series. The other five were written by Larry Stevens, Spike Milligan and I think Eric Sykes was involved. By now we'd established a complete working rapport with Hancock. But we were still very young, you see, and that's why they wouldn't entrust us with all eight of the first series of 'Forces' All Star Bill'. And also from Tony's point of view — he was the star and he'd been working with Larry Stevens for a long time, and it served as a kind of insurance policy for him.

How did the radio Half Hour evolve out of that?

Galton   Well that show continued, though with different titles, for about another three years. Which took us up to 1954.

Simpson   During that time, we were writing for practically every comic in the country, because they were coming on the show as guests. And we also used to try to get a lot of big names in terms of straight acting to do guest appearances. We wrote a hell of a lot of shows and I think it was during that period that we learned how to write, really learned our trade.

So you were ready for a move in a new direction?

Simpson   Yes. Well the ultimate to our mind, and I think to Tony's mind, was to get away from the 'And now it's Eddie Calvert . . . the man with the golden trumpet'. To get away from the Variety type set up and do a situation comedy. We went to the BBC with Tony to say what about doing a situation comedy. And Dennis Main Wilson, who was still producing 'All Star Bill', was all for it. We didn't know this until the recent 'Celebration' programme, but Dennis said he had a terrible job selling the idea to the BBC. They didn't want to know about it. But finally they agreed to do it.

Galton The idea was that we wanted to do a half-hour situation comedy without funny voices and without jokes as such. The humour was to come out of the situation. Tony was in complete agreement and so was Dennis.

Had you thought out what form this would take?

Simpson The format we were after was a storyline not split up at all by other acts. Just go straight the way through like a half-hour play.

Galton We also knew that we wanted Sid James, for instance. We didn't know his name, but we wanted him. We said, 'We've seen a bloke in the Alec Guiness film The Lavender Hill Mob, we don't know his name, but he'd be ideal'. So we went to see the film again — 'That's him, that's the fellow' — looked on the credits, Sidney James. So we approached Sid and he was terrified, he'd never worked on radio before. Absolutely terrified. But in the end he was persuaded with money to do it. I always remember Sid during the first few shows — he used to wear a trilby with the brim pulled right down over his eyes, because he was scared stiff of looking at the audience. So much so that he couldn't keep his script still, it'd be shaking away, making a terrible noise. He then tried putting it on a music stand, and unclipping it all so it was all in single pages. But he abandoned that idea after the stand collapsed in the middle of a broadcast and his script went floating off in all directions. Another piece of inspired casting came from Dennis Main Wilson when he suggested Kenneth Williams, whom he had just seen play the Dauphin on the stage in Shaw's *St Joan*.

Simpson We started the show with Tony, playing the character Tony Hancock as he was at that stage of development. But for a half an hour situation comedy you have to have other people to bounce off. We decided on a criminal element, which was Sid James, the shady friend who was going to get into trouble all the time. We'd known Bill Kerr almost since we came into the business and we thought he'd be very good as another element, a sort of idiot, you know, where Tony was superior to him, so we could also play those two against each other. Also we needed a female — in those days you had to have a female element. And we were already working in the 'Star Bill' series with Moira Lister. So she came in as Tony's unspecified girl friend. That was the only role that changed. The 'Half Hour' started with Moira Lister, then André Melly, and then Hattie Jacques. And Hattie stayed with the radio show right to the end.
We were under contract at this stage to the BBC. We had signed a three-year contract, which we thought was fantastic, in 1952. They guaranteed us work of twenty shows a year with a first year fee of 60 guineas for the hour, 65 guineas in the second year, and 70 guineas in the third. Both 'Star Bill' and 'Hancock's Half Hour' came in under the contract. And when that was finished in 1955, we'd written one series of Hancock. The contract lapsed and we went freelance.

Did Hancock have any influence over your writing for the radio series?

Galton Well we created it but Hancock did have a say in it. He never liked to rest on laurels and was always looking for change in his characterisation. He wanted an advancement of character, to get closer and closer to reality.

But despite this, you kept to a standard format for approximately 100 radio shows.

Simpson You've got to bear in mind that now we're talking about doing a series of 20 shows a time. So consequently you're faced with 20 weeks on the trot. The basic conception of the show was a situation comedy right through. But occasionally during the series we'd decide to do something different. For instance, we did The Moon and Tuppence Halfpenny, which was three sketches of Somerset Maugham's type of setting, out in Malaya with the rubber plantations.

Galton Some weeks we did those kind of shows out of sheer desperation because we couldn't think of anything.

Simpson We did the East Cheam rep a couple of times.

How did Railway Cuttings and East Cheam evolve?

Galton Originally I suppose with Hancock's character — we decided to make a failed theatrical. Though we weren't specific as to whether he was a Shakespearean actor, or a comedian. We seemed to lean more towards the failed Shakespearean. But it wasn't consistent, and neither was his fortune. Some weeks Sid would be conning him out of a few thousand, and other weeks he'd be broke. So it was a gradual emphasis towards reality. It didn't happen at once. We were making our way towards more real situations over the years.

Simpson The basic character really, from the show business point of view, was that at this stage in his career he'd been forced into doing this comic-ing and working in tatty rep companies. According to Hancock the character Laurence Olivier and Gielgud are where they are purely by chance. He should have been there really. He would defend it, as well, by saying 'If they're so good, let them play Scunthorpe on a Saturday afternoon and see how they get on.'

What about the name — Anthony Aloysius St John Hancock?

Galton Purely pretentiousness on his part. This was why we chose East Cheam. To us in those days Cheam was the epitome of upper-class suburbia, the Beverley Hills of South London. And so we thought we'd put him there. But obviously he couldn't really be there otherwise he'd be quite rich, so we put him in East Cheam, which was not quite Cheam. And there again Railway Cuttings, that made a visual picture of a grimey Victorian terrace.

Simpson As for the name, he was obviously asked at some stage of a show to fill out a form to get a visa or passport or something — and they'd say, 'Name', and rather than say Tony Hancock he'd say, 'Anthony Hancock' and then 'Anthony Aloysius St John Hancock'. He also used to get very annoyed if anyone called him 'Tone'. We never actually ascertained in the scripts whether Anthony Aloysius St John was his real name or whether that was just him putting on the dog. But after a time everybody started calling him that — the press and the public.

What conditioned the change from radio to television?

Simpson Well the first thing about conditioning the change was that in those days nobody wanted to go on television, because it was the poor relation. You couldn't earn the money on television for a start. If an artist went on television he immediately — a top artist — cut his money right down.

Galton Because he couldn't do the Halls then, you see. He'd be working all week rehearsing, whereas a radio show was strictly a Sunday afternoon or any afternoon that the artist could fit in.

Simpson Also the fees they got on radio, with the repeats, were probably twice as much. We could have gone on television much earlier,

but Hancock didn't want to. Everything was fine about television apart from the finances of it. The situation changed when the ITV started, because they started paying out money. We were offered money to write for ITV which was twice what we'd ever been offered. Hancock went straight on to ITV, his first television was in 1955 for Jack Hylton.

Galton But he was trying to work off a stage contract. He was very anti-stage at that time and he had this contract with Hylton, who offered to scrub the contract if he did the television series. So Hancock agreed. As we were still under contract to the BBC at that time we couldn't write it. The shows were not going too well and they approached us again. The BBC said they'd turn a blind eye to our writing it but we couldn't put our names on it.

Simpson But the money they were paying was incredible. That was the biggest money we had ever earned, doing a couple of sketches for Tony's ITV series. This was in 1955, so when 1956 came round everybody thought 'Let's get on the television now,' you know, 'there's money to be earned'.

So then it was time for the transition of the radio half hour to TV.

Simpson Yes. I think Hancock, having experienced television was now prepared to have a crack. And also the BBC in 1956 had started to compete in terms of the money they paid.

Galton It was proved to be more than just an adjunct to radio. It was proved to be a very viable proposition.

Simpson Tony and ourselves decided that we would have a go and transfer 'Hancock's Half Hour' to television. Then it got down to deciding whether it was going to be a straight transformation of the radio show, from the cast point of view.

Galton Which we felt couldn't work. We wanted to concentrate mainly on the relationship between Tony and Sid James.

Simpson In those days, television was quite crude, and it was all done live. What would take 30 minutes to do with four people and various situations on a radio show, would take 45 or 50 minutes to do on television. You can't have a regular cast without using them all the time, so we narrowed it down to just two.

Can you remember the very first television shows?

Simpson The first one we did was a very trady thing about Hancock being given a television show, and he's all ready to make his name in television and he falls down and breaks his leg. But the people at the BBC insist he goes on, you know, 'I'm sorry, you've had your money'. 'I cannot work with my leg in plaster.' 'I'm sorry, you've had your money and it's got to be done.'

Galton 'Show's got to go on.'

Simpson And so he played the whole show with his leg in plaster. In the hospital bed with the scenery being put round it. And from there he did a sketch about Nelson.

Can you briefly describe the development of the series until it was Hancock alone?

Galton Well, as I say, Hancock was not one for standing still. He wanted change, change, change. As far as it was possible. He did get a little weary of what he thought was a Laurel and Hardy relationship between he and Sid, and the feeling that he couldn't appear without Sid James. It wasn't a double act as far as he was concerned — he was a comedian in his own right and he used to appear on the stage without Sid, and so really I suppose he wanted to prove that he was an individual. Also at the time, he wanted to become an international star, which really meant becoming known in America. And he thought the astrakhan coat and the East Cheam set-up were too parochial, and the slang, and so we gradually dropped these facets of his character.

What were your own feelings about this?

Galton   Oh, we were in agreement.

Simpson   Well we were certainly in agreement with the reason for doing the show without Sid. I don't think one ever really felt that he was right about trying to Americanise himself. Not Americanise himself — de-Englishise himself, if you like. He never did, you know.

A number of the programmes in which he was by himself seem to have stuck as the classic Hancock.

Simpson   Yes. It's a strange dichotomy because people still, even today, say that he was never the same after he left Sid James. Even now.

Galton   Because they still think that Sid was in those. They think that Sid James was in The Blood Donor, they think he was in The Radio Ham, they think he was in The Lift. It's because we only did six programmes. If we'd gone on to do another series then they would have realised.

Another mystique which seems to have also developed is that Hancock in the television programmes was very much Hancock the person.

Galton   Well this is a case of . . .

Simpson   The brilliance of the writers!

Galton   . . . trying to achieve some sort of reality.

There is, for example, his personal yearning for knowledge — a desire to know more about philosophy etc. and, as if to parallel this, your programme of him alone trying to read Bertrand Russell.

Simpson   That was taking the piss out of Hancock and ourselves, at the time.

Galton   Because we met quite often socially, and did discuss politics and philosophy and religion and rubbish like that all through the night. We all felt basically the same about these things. I suppose we were all left-wing, non-believers as far as religion goes and reasonably pessimistic about the human condition.

Simpson   We all must have been very arrogant, but with the saving grace of a sense of humour about it. The Bertrand Russell bit, and loads of other little bits in there were examples of deflating ourselves, really. Which is the great thing about English humourists.

What actually led to the breakdown of your relationship with Hancock?

Galton   Well it began after the first film we wrote for Hancock, *The Rebel*. It was a financial success and it wasn't a bad film considering it was his first one, and no comic had really made the transition from radio and television on to the big screen. I don't know why, to this day, but it's a very difficult thing to do. Hancock certainly wanted the second one to be an international film and we were writing it. We would agree on the subject matter and he'd say 'Right, well OK that's fine'. We wrote three altogether.

Simpson   The first two he never read, just said that he didn't like the idea, he'd gone off it, and the third time we said 'Well look, don't ring us up three weeks into writing. Wait until the script's finished and then read it.' And so that's what he did. And he read it and didn't like it. So by that time we'd spent about four or five months without any money, and we decided we had to earn some. He agreed and said 'Well why don't you do some television and earn some money and I'll think about the film and then we'll get together in a few months' time.' And we did that and of course 'Steptoe and Son' emerged.

Galton   But by that time he had gone back to an idea for a film that we had all discussed anyway. And he said 'All right, I'll pursue that idea,' and he and Philip Oakes wrote *The Punch and Judy Man*.

Which in fact, in terms of his image, was very parochial.

Galton Very much so. But I think Hancock emerged out of it as a better actor and had he lived I think he could have gone on to be a great comic actor.

But as far as Hancock himself was concerned, you must have been aware of his apparent mental and physical breakdown.

Galton Well it gets a bit personal I suppose, things one doesn't really want to talk about. One thing that did happen, he had a car crash which put him back rehearsal-wise and he couldn't learn the script in time, so nearly all the words were written on idiot boards. And that was for The Blood Donor, and if you look at it now you'll see that he's not looking at June Whitfield or anyone else — he's looking over their shoulder and he's reading it all. And he thought, 'This is marvellous, isn't it? Why have I been flogging my guts out for the last ten years or so learning all these scripts, when you can do it this way?' So he continued like that.

Simpson The last three of the series were read. And then the split came over the film thing and then he went over to ITV and did a series there, and again read them all. Sometimes when an actor reads his part instead of learning it the naturalness of the performance suffers. Certainly he never seemed quite the same after that. Anyway we didn't have anything to do with him after '61 but we met him about three or four times in '61 to '68, when he died.

If Hancock were alive, would you still like to be writing for him?

Galton It's mind bending to think that we could have been writing it since '54. I think that's too terrifying to think of.

Simpson But I think there's no doubt that if he was alive and in the same mental and physical condition as he was at his peak, probably about 1959, 1960, he'd still be the top man.

If you look back on specifically the television programmes, which ones do you recall with a particular sense of creative satisfaction?

Galton I think three or four of the six we wrote for him in the last series, The Blood Donor, and The Lift, and Hancock Alone. Which was a big breakthrough because we did that deliberately. After the dropping of Sid James everybody was saying 'Ah now we'll see, now we'll see.' So we deliberately made the show so that he was not just without Sid James, he was without any support whatsoever. That was our decision and we asked him and he said, 'Yeah, do it'.

Simpson I'll always remember taking the script to Shrewsbury. He was doing a variety season up there and he hadn't seen the script. He didn't even know he was going to be alone. We took it up to him — pages and pages of it — instructions, which we'd never really done before, as opposed to dialogue. We were worried about it because it was a complete break, and we thought he'd say 'Oh no, I can't do this'. Of course as soon as he saw it . . . it must have been a great ego-boost, you know, half an hour entirely on his own, and he said 'Marvellous, brilliant'. It was a chance, but of course he loved it — the idea of doing it. Even if it had been a terrible script I'm sure he would have gone on and done it.